GOOD SUCCESS

GOOD SUCCESS

❖ Visions and Legacies that Last ❖

Metashar Dillon

Order this book online at www.trafford.com
or email orders@trafford.com

Most Trafford titles are also available at major online book retailers.

Printed in the United States of America.

ISBN: 978-1-4669-4222-6 (sc)
ISBN: 978-1-4669-4223-3 (e)

Trafford rev. 09/20/2012

   www.trafford.com

North America & international
toll-free: 1 888 232 4444 (USA & Canada)
phone: 250 383 6864 ♦ fax: 812 355 4082

CONTENTS

THE MESSAGE

Good Success comes from creating an idea and or discovering a need. You must ponder and meditate on your ideas all day and night, making sure you practice everything written in it. Then you'll get where you're going; then you'll succeed. Strength! Courage! Don't be timid; don't get discouraged. Yes just do it!

Who should read this book?

For so long, many have not been able to define "what I like" versus "what I was born to do" in this earth, and how to really measure "Good Success". This book is intended to outline how you measure your success, how to set goals and get them accomplished, and have a balanced life with God, Family, and Friends. How you can leave legacies that will continue to affect your community that will spread into the global market and benefit all of humanity by leaving positive legacies on the earth. The important keys to remember to accomplish "Good Success" are:

Vast Wealth of Information and Knowledge

In a practical sense, I believe that wealth and prosperity are no accident but are created by design. What I intend to outline here is a practical approach to creating wealth. You need to accomplish God's vision for you. I have lived with these principles for years and they can be applied to every level of wealth you aspire to have. These principles should be used and adhered to. More of these details can be found in the famous book,[1] "The Richest Man in Babylon", whose timeless messages apply to us today. Be it a small/large business owner or the leader of an organization, global company and or mega-church, your survival and prosperity growth depend on it. So the question is how do we get started on a path to prosperity? The urgency of change comes from your desire for the compassion of all of mankind to be evident in your life. These elements are peace, love, and prosperity. To have these, we must use all of the resources that are apparent and those that are not. What I mean is that the beginning of wisdom comes from understanding that God, who is of infinite intelligence, gives to his children an abundance of knowledge and information to create and command their future. Specifically, God requires us to walk and act intelligently with the care and concern of all humanity in mind, as we build and leave legacies that will last.

We must tap into this vast resource to get and make the unimaginable ideas and thoughts of reality in the very existence of our representation of what we all were created to do in our boundary of time we have on earth. Take for instance our ability to communicate face to face to anyone around the world in real time. This idea or thought was transmuted into the mind and heart of man. In this vast resource of infinite wisdom and mind of God are the solutions to your situation and problems (opportunities for God to show himself). He is ready to release these as we walk into the untapped resource. Have you ever prayed, and then suddenly had a dream or a "hunch" of a new approach to solving a problem? God is transmiting new ideas and strategies to you. Don't just brush these off. Have you ever asked God for a solution, and saw an advertisement of a new product that fit perfectly? Have you ever had an idea that you knew would be revolutionary and delayed moving out on securing this idea in the marketplace, and eventually saw it being sold and offered to the public? As created beings, we get the insight and foresight of things to come. God said that nothing on earth would come to pass unless it would be revealed unto us.

Thus, begin with the spiritual understanding of the massive energy God has stored up for us to help us create a compelling vision. Don't worry that you don't have all the answers, but know that God will pour out these answers to you liberally. You may have prayed in the past for solutions that took time, months/years/decades, for God to answer. But I pray that the "now", suddenly is going to happen for you! Believe that it will be released in your life through these words. Reframe your words (and questions for God) for specific solutions to specific problems. Use your words to describe what the solution looks like, and reflect, meditate, upon this regularly. Act! Here lies the abundance of new ideas and opportunities for God's greatness to be reflected in our lives.

Eliminate Excuses

So with the knowledge of the vast storehouses of resources that already exist, there is no end to what will be reveal to you. As you read these words, recall what ideas have already been put into your spirit. Is it a new invention? Go patent it. Is it a solution for someone else's dilemma? Go share it, in the wisdom of God. Is it a new business or concept to revolutionize an old one? Get help in writing the business plan. *MIND* your own business!!! The message here is action, no more delays.

There will always be a reason or some excuse about why you can't and many road blocks that will get in your way to try and discouraged you. If you make up your mind and settle in your heart, you will begin to see more of the positive rather than the negative. It is then that you will begin to move forward to position yourself for "Good Success"! But always remember God knows everyone and above the thought of any man, he knows that you are and were created just for this job that you are about to create.

Some of the most successful people that have moved into the place of Legacy stakeholders in the past lacked some self-confidence. They are human and so are you. What they had was faith in God to move obstacles out of the way and provide the resources and talent to accomplish the mission. What do you see as challenges to your vision? What distraction have you intentionally (or unintentionally) placed in front of your mirror? Imagine these as nothing but dust or smears on your mirror. As you set out to clean up your vision and your reflection, ask God to remove away anything that is not like him. Is there anything too hard for God?

Decision

The evidence of a true decision to change is followed by actions. Often we decide to change our situation be it through the inspired word of God or the desperation of a tragic event. Either inspiration or desperation are helpful catalysts for change. But what happens when you are not inspired or desperate enough to consider change?

We see here that God is not interested in the status quo. He is interested in getting the most out of our lives and his creation. Look around. Are you a constant agent of change to the lives around you? Do you have a passion for your fellow man in making their lives better? What is the legacy that you plan to leave for the next generation?

You must understand that since the great depression things have been happening in cycles because of man. You must make a decision and change your thinking. Make up your own mind to reposition yourself for "Good Success".

Courage and Faith That Works

Most of us have heard the expression "ACTIONS SPEAK LOUDER THAN WORDS" and, whether you agree or not, decision and action plays a vital role in achieving greatness. Imagine if some of the brightest women and men in the world held their ideas to themselves and shared them with only a few people. Action in this sense is intended to describe the step that follows decision. You must have (or build) the faith or courage necessary to carry out the mission whether you have decided to make the shifts necessary to change your future, or whether God has inspired you with new instructions. What is faith? Faith is an action word, which is a verb that describes movement, doing something that will cause activity. God asks us to rely on it, as without it, it is impossible to have good success and you will never be happy within you and will never fulfill the legacy.

Here are some practical faith action steps to prioritize the numerous ideas and get started on this journey.

1. **Look for the need**. What has been done within you for you to be at this point in your life right now, for you to have a need to want look at your surroundings and do something about them? You have a created a unique element in His "Periodic Table of Elements" that only your individual uniqueness can best serve and benefit all of humanity. Shortfalls that you see in your family, community, globally, church or organization are voids that need filling. Often at times we label our brothers and sisters as rebellious when they offer different ideas from our own, but these individuals have added insights that should be embraced and used for people. They will add experiences that could give us the edge we need. They add to the team's dynamics that should be utilized and viewed as valid solutions to the cause. View these voids as areas you can serve in your current capacity to shore up the cause that can cause you to do your part while you're here on earth. Understand that these business ideas are voids in the marketplace to fill a niche or need.

2. **Start by collecting** all of the ideas that you have pondered over the years for other ways to create wealth. If it is a business idea or vision, where have you seen the shortfall of the faith that seems to give you the greatest heartburn? Is it the lack of brotherly love, or charity? These challenges are not unique but should be solved and shared with the masses. When you have something great to do as my mentor directed me over 15 years ago, "all the wealth that is going to be entrusted to you is because you are going to empower people" was the reason I collected knowledge to benefit others besides myself.

3. **Work in this capacity** with all of your heart and soul. As you exert energy in improving the marketplace, community, organization, or body at your local church, it will catch on. Research and find, or ask God for creative ways to market your new position or product. Get help. Communicate the vision of the new idea at every level or opportunity. Create a powerful alliance or network of like-minded individuals to continue to develop and promote it.

4. **Ensure that your position or product adds value.** If it is for your community, a global market place, organization or in your local church, it should be in line with the vision of that venue or you should have an analysis done to find out the direction you need to go. If it is in the market place, seek advice from experienced individuals in this field. Look for ways to improve the product, cost to market, and differentiation to similar products. Reframe your view of the marketplace as necessary to institute new improvements. You are one idea (thought) away from

changing your destiny. For leaders, embrace new and innovative ways to solve your problems. You have prayed, so know that God will send the answer.

5. **Get expert help when you need it.** Not all problems are new problems in the big picture.

This is the faith that works. This is the faith that transforms [2]"intangible ideas into tangible realities." One other point to mention here is the influence of the concept of time management. Be aware of the use of time, every decision to act, every milestone or goal should have your commitment on when it will be achieved. God has the best of the best stored for us.

Legacies That Last

[3] *"A good man leaves an inheritance [of moral stability and goodness] to his children's children, and the wealth.*

A good life gets passed on to the grandchildren; ill-gotten wealth ends up with good people."

The best conclusion to one's compelling vision is measured by its ability to influence the next generation (grandchildren). God wants your seed and so does the enemy. You will leave a legacy. The question is: will it die after one generation or fade as a freshly plucked flower? Will the next generation celebrate and remember you? We so often forget to document the life and legacy of our lives and leave our children with a clear understanding of their lineage. We find ourselves asking, "Who am I, what is my purpose, what is my destiny?" Have you found yourself around people that just want you to help them with their destiny and now your eyes are open and you realize you haven't done anything towards your own destiny. Have you struggled with defining your legacy? The answers to these life-long questions are found in knowing more of the legacy left for us and our challenge to sustain that legacy. Begin to be the catalyst and start pioneering the start of a new ground breaking of "what about my own legacy". Deal with reconciling what has been given and taken to where it is sustainable for future generations. It is much easier for us to stand on the shoulders of the giants that have come before us than for every generation to rediscover itself. We lose time and energy re-defining who we are because we lack the often unwritten information from our forefathers.

We have written documents of God's plan for man from the beginning of time to the end. There are countless studies that describe the plan of God unto why man was even created and the likeness of whom he was created like and what man is most likely created to be doing on earth. Throughout the historical books, there is a written testament of this plan and it is played out through documented accounts of the lives of successful people and their contributions to His plan. It describes countless challenges placed before man and how they overcame these challenges. God spoke to men of old and told them of His legacy and that His seed would be greater than the sand on the shore and stars in the heavens. There are many stories written of many detailed accounts of the lives of people's accomplishments that we can read about in times past and garner inspiration to overcome any obstacles in our lives.

How wonderful would it be for your children and their children to read of your accomplishments and relate them to their struggles? How important is it to you that your lineage is not lost as many have been lost before you. What untold advantages will your children have from first understanding what you accomplished and how you accomplished it? What wisdom will they have as an advantage over other children/people around them? Most importantly, the failures you endured and recovered from should be marked as learning experiences not to be repeated. For the Bible says that the very iniquity that plagued you will be revisited to your children, and your children's children. Your legacy will help to identify these pitfalls. Your triumphs over addictions and drugs, your darkest days, are all learning experiences destined to be repeated by your children unless the vicious cycle is broken. Leave a legacy that will last or your seed will just have to figure it out on their own. Empower your next generation to stand on your shoulders and reach heights that you did not. Give them an advantage to overcome the world and provide a path for their accomplishments by leaving a written legacy that will last, or document how the wealth was acquired with instructions, so that the wealth will remain, and continue to grow leaving legacies for all humanity.

Develop Proper Discipline

The consequences of good discipline are far reaching in mental, physical, and spiritual. Sound mental acumen requires the development of your spiritual gifts. As you go through life, you have learned to discern behaviors of people around you who mean you no good. We have made good decisions and bad decisions. The key here is to reflect on all these decisions, especially the bad ones, whose lessons were painful to bear. Their lessons are even painful to reflect on. But, we must look at these decisions, their consequences and learn from them.

Get fit. The weight of responsibility is heavy, and it takes sacrifice. It requires long, extensive work habits as when you began to teach your young child how to walk. You must develop "Good Success" habits not only to bear the weight of responsibility, but also the physical wear and tear on your body. With enthusiasm and zeal, it requires a substantial amount of physical endurance habits to get the job done. Apply the passion of "Good Success" habits to maintaining a healthy lifestyle.

Not enough can be said about seeking first the kind of character building you need, and making sure you are equipped, rooted and have taken your own assessment for your journey. We have an accountability to people for the role that we play while we exist here on earth. So, settle your life. Discipline yourself so you can find out what you are going to be doing with the latter part of your life in order that you may be remembered in the history notes of your generation and all of mankind to come for "Good Success".

Value Time

You must respect time. Time is finite in regards to a person's time on earth. Understand that time will continue to move and we need to capture it while it's in the initial value problem of the time domain. It is designed to have movement for that specific boundary within that time and space that is given. Whatever you do within your infinite wisdom given to you by God, you must remember that there is a boundary by which you have to get your legacy done called valued time.

"Good Success" will bring and promote:
Education reformation
Social Reconstruction
Community Development
Political Enfranchisement
Economic Movement
Spiritual Renewal
Day change Liberation

BIOGRAPHY

Metashar Bankhead Dillon

MRS. METASHAR BANKHEAD Dillon was elected Chairman, Kingdom International Economic Development Corporation. She works as Owner Operator of Executive Touch Spa and Salon, Farmington, Connecticut, USA, and Co-owner of California Hair Designs, Hamden, Connecticut, USA. She is the founder and Executive Director of the Miss Black Connecticut Scholarship Pageant that has given out numerous scholarship awards for higher education. She is a fourth generation entrepreneur. Since 2000 she has been holding statewide food and resource rally's to help people statewide and aboard. She has received many awards from government officials throughout her lifetime, and in 2009 she was awarded the Community action award from the Alpha Kappa Alpha Sorority. In 2010, KIEDC held its kickoff of "Boomin" 2010 event in Bushnell Park, Hartford Connecticut. This event featured free and informational services for the people of Connecticut ranging from food, clothes, medical services, to Bank mortgage assistance from the great loss of homes. In 2011 she was awarded the Connie Wilson Collins Award from The NAACP. In 2011 she received an award as one of the top 100 Most Influential Blacks in Connecticut. In 2011 she offered free hair grooming services to the community, "Haircuts/Styles for Jobs, for jobless individuals because of the economic hit to Connecticut. She is known nationally and internationally for her divine insights, and highly gifted with expertise for insights in the area of the market place for economics and entrepreneurship. She speaks regularly across the nation and the world, transforming and empowering people to bring change to nations in the area of economics leaving legacies that will last and that will benefit all of humanity.

She has attended many training and educational platforms from the Broadcasting School of Connecticut, Los Angeles Trade and Technical Institute, The Contemporary School of Beauty, Kingdom University, the Economic Development Leadership and Training, Training for the Cultivation of Women, Bank Boston/Gateway, and University of Hartford Women's College Business Entrepreneurial and Technical programs.

She is the president of Kingdom International Economic Development Corporation (KIEDC, www.KIEDC.com). KIEDC is a non-profit foundation formed that builds on a commitment to deliver socio-economic change that will bring hope to benefit all of humanity and several for profit businesses. She is the Author of the published book "The Power of Vision and The Reflection of your Future"

She has visited many nations and countries serving as a humanitarian in many capacities, a renowned public speaker, and a great community activist. Her most well-known strength is being very gifted by God and having insights. She assists Community leaders around the nation in developing a sound road map with shovel-ready projects that will help individuals, as well as benefit all of humanity, along with one on one training lessons delivered onsite and coaching for groups of business entrepreneurs. She has been in business since the age of 18, and has counseled many leaders, businesswomen/men, and entrepreneurs, and many goal medalist professionals in every capacity, and just ordinary people in new and already existing businesses and projects with divine insights on how to start, how to expand and make a new start, with God given insights of expertise for "Good Success". She also coaches women to help prepare them for adoption to help babies. The desire of Metashar's heart is for people of all nations to be empowered in the area of economics and the marketplace and begin to leave legacies on the earth that will last and change their current state of being to bring about change to all of humanity which will bring "Good Success".

DEDICATION

To my God whom I serve for allowing me to be earmarked for bringing change, to have compassion, for all people, whose lives this will touch, I dedicate this book to you. In memory of my Grandmother Etta Brown Bromell who was a gracious woman, who had a word of wisdom to whom all that came in contact with her, my loving mother, Estelle Barfield, who is my trumpeter, that sowed the seed of entrepreneurship in my life at an early age, the reason for me being in this place of Business even now, all of my powerful aunts, and women that have touched my life, even in this new decade.

Especially to some powerful women of God that have also impacted my life journey and that helped me get where I am going. That spoke into my life that the fruit will always remain, Dr. Marie Tremble, Dr. Kim CarMicheal, Dr. Cindy Trimm, Dr. Bernice Gibbs, Dr. Violet Burns, Dr. Pam Vinnett, Pastor Faye August, Prayer Generals: Kim Woolnough, Amber Estes, Victoria Gordon, Chandra Winfred, Mother Charles Etta Ingram, Mother Marilyn Liggins, Mother Elizabeth McClary, Mother Bessie Carrington, Mother Olivia Monk, Jean Blake Jackson, Judy Young, and memory of Dr. Vinnest Hardy. My sisters Thelma Barfield, Thomasina Wearing, Ivy Young, Terri Jones and Dr. Andrea Toulson Jeffress.

ACKNOWLEDGEMENTS

I give God the glory. Thanks to my loving husband, for being my eagle, my friend, my love of my life Wesley J. Dillon, my family and mentors especially the men that have been placed in my life, Elder Marlon Reid, Dr. Aubrey Shines, that have sowed so much in my life, All of my special Uncles, and Pastor Reginald Rice. Also to my Pastor Dr. John E. Wilson, who has believed God for my life and in memory of my late Grandfather Abraham Bromell.

My two sons: Thomas and Chase.

Thank you

I would like to say a special thank you to two powerful "Good Successful" women.

Editors: Naomi Kilgore, Executive Secretary, and Nicole Rodriguez, Executive Assistant, for coming into my life, by divine destiny for such a time as this. Thank you!

INTRODUCTION

WHEN I WAS born as the second child of three siblings, my dad and mom were both shot at the same time, my dad in the heart and mom in the groin. My father died from the injury. My mother was pregnant with my youngest sister and survived. So, we have a young woman with three small children. She had a wonderful family and a mother and father who helped her as her life took a change. Fortunately, our dad had great work ethics and was not a lazy man. He built bridges and helped design the very infrastructure we use to this day to travel on to Charleston, SC. However, he left some substance that he was able to make sure his children had the necessary things to survive he was responsible man, even from the ground. My mother found herself, having to go into the workforce to help take care of her children. She later had another battle with death when a doctor took her into an operation room and operated without permission and left her with poison running through her body to die. A nurse found her and the hospital had to get a court order from the court to do emergency surgery in order to try and save her. She was in the mercy of God again, asking and praying to please save me so that I can raise my children. She made some more promises to the Lord that I will let her tell you about in her volume of books of the miracles of her life. Well, it was a distraction and a very devastating event that took place then in California. I remember a nurse calling our home for her. My mom and my sister were talking on the phone and I started crying saying "What's wrong with my mommy", as my mom was giving her instructions to call someone to get us to the hospital. I remember my family coming from all over to visit and help with us, again faced with death, but God intervened. We didn't see my mommy for months. Finally, our family took us to the hospital to see her. When she rose again, she went back to school to be retrained. I then found out that she was going to be a hair stylist and business owner.

What seemed to be so bad actually turned around for our family to continue the legacy that would last. She became a business owner in 1975 and has been one since. What seemed to be the worst time of our lives ended up being the greatest so that we all could have great, "Good Success". My grandparents and their father started by buying the land and establishing a foundation that would last a lifetime. They were store owners, farmers and had other small businesses such as trucking companies, tree Bumper Company, tractor trailer and two bus line franchises.

The moral of "Good Success" is that you cannot be lazy, look for handouts you must have good work ethics. The introduction to getting started is some people have a platform to leap from and some don't. However, whatever position you find yourself in, you can get started by writing down the vision, make it plain so that others may follow it and bring it to life. As I was growing up, I inherited one of the businesses in California at the age of eighteen. I didn't think I knew enough to take over, but I did. I thought I did not have the capacity to run the business when my mother went to open up her second salon. I had to get it up and running. I realized that I did know more than I gave myself credit for. I realized that I had to trust God for the insight and I had a mentor, my mother that I could call and ask for advice from time to time. My mom had prepared us all. She used to travel all over the country for her clients, so we had to run things around the home front and the business. When we were kids, mom was training us how to run a business and deal with people when we were sweeping the floor and answering the phone. Ten years after mom started her business chain of salons and traveling stylist. I was in a position to transition and become an entrepreneur at the age of eighteen. I was running the salon in Gardena, California while my mom was opening her second salon on the east coast in Connecticut. We were able to continue learning even as we matured and became wiser. My mom opened the third salon in Norwalk, Connecticut. The demand was greater on the east coast for us than on the west coast. I transitioned to the east coast where the demand was. As my sister and I worked with my mom, the storm of life came in 1988 when a tornado blew our neighborhood down and we lost everything except our lives. At that location, not by the storm alone, but because situation of devastation laws were not put into effect just yet, the officials demolished what we could had saved and crushed our thriving business, cars, etc. We had to start over again. Then we had a second storm. We had only had the computer for about five months with our faithful clients.

So in the midst, God prevailed. New laws were made to protect victims of disasters and we reopened our business. So, God would always give us "Good Success". After running a thirty-five year old business, we not only could talk about entrepreneurship, but also our track record of knowing how to be sustainable speaks for it self. We now have the credentials of the intellect and the experience of the tangible testimony of the applicable hands on experience. We have a track record of how to and what not to do in good times and bad, while always learning, as such as life is, "Good Success".

A legacy was passed from Grandmother Etta and Abraham Bromell, to my mom down to my generation was that of good work ethics and entrepreneurship. The torch is still lit. My mom's birth children are all entrepreneurs and are presently in business and have been for the last 35 years.

"Good Success"—Insights into the Heart of God
The Oil Well

One day, I woke up and the phone rang. It was one of my mentors, an old prayer warrior in about her late seventies at the time. Whenever someone needed counseling or needed answers, people all around the world would call this elder, especially when they were in trouble and could not see a way to escape. This powerful woman in her own right never really got the recognition she deserved, but her rewards in her later life would be greater than her former, when she got to heaven. But people who knew her and of her, either knew how to contact her personally or knew someone else who knew how to contact her, all times of day and night. Well, I answered the call. "Hello mother, how are you" she answered "Fine and you", and then she said, "I don't want to say too much, but I have a young man on the phone with me, and I am too close to the situation. I need you to pray for him right now." I knew what that meant, not to talk any more. We are trained that when there is a 911 call in progress, it means man can't do what needs to be done on the earth, but we aren't talking anymore in the natural means by informed information or by the hands of human beings. This is where the unseen things, our belief that nothing on the earth will ever come to pass except until it is revealed first unto his servants. When you are counseling someone, you need to talk it out, but he wasn't calling for us to counsel him. Mother already did that without me on the phone. Now, this man needed answers, a miracle was needed. I began praying for him and all I could speak out was "restoration and you will have "Good Success", that what you tried to do on your own and that which was taken shall be returned unto you." "I am the Lord your God and I am taking my hand underneath the earth and causing the oil to come to the surface. What man can't do I will do it" saith God, "tell him to go to his property in three days and he will see that I am God. You have lost all that you had, but I will restore you." Well, by the time I was finished praying, the man was in awe, one because I did not have any information, no knowledge about his present nor his past situation. He was weeping because of the place of hardship. If you haven't ever been in this place, you really can't understand the position of this man's 911 problem. He needed a solution. I later found out that this man had lost millions on top of millions of dollars trying to get this oil pumped by engineers with heavy equipment in the ground. "It's like I know that it is there but I can't seem to pin point and put my hands on the target done by the experts." Three days later, the man could not get to the land on his own because his resources were really tight. He lived in California. He finally got his answer. Years of losing all of his investments, God stuck his hand on the earth, and the oil came up and was going all over the property. This was the real life observation taken by the groundkeepers when they got to the oil site. Oil was coming up from everywhere! When I got the call later with the results, I said, "No matter what it looks like, He wants you to have "Good Success", to prosper, even as your soul prospers." People always want to know, how we know these things. I always say, "I don't know these things but they are revealed unto me." This life has been a building block that speaks into people's lives from all walks of life to have "Good Success". This was a "Good Success" story of a man with a promise for his destiny.

The Promise that was made

A divinely connected friend of mine has many stories to share. We have shared many of them over the past decades. This friend called me with a friend on the phone from Detroit and, I not only prayed for him, but watched his life. He has battled many different events in his life, but triumphed over them all. It was about twenty years ago, that God brought us together. He was born to do what we are watching come to pass in the fullness of time. This is the promise that his feet would be in a large place and his purpose of what he was born to do was made known. He would become the ambassador of the television media kingdom. He is the largest African American television owner in the United States. I sat and participated as a prayer vessel and as a mouthpiece to oversee it in the prevision of earth's manifestation, as a reminder of a promise knowing what God had spoken on several events. "That the table would turn around for him, and he would have "Good Success"". He now owns over 27 television stations and networks and operates out of 65 different markets. There is a time and season for everything. Ponder and meditate on it day and night, making sure you practice everything written in it. Then you'll get where you're going and succeed. "Haven't I commanded you? Strength! Courage! Don't be timid, don't get discouraged." God your God is with you every step you take. God takes nothing and makes something. He comes that you have "Good Success". This is the greatest time right now if you can grab a hold of it for "Good Success".

I prayed a prayer one day and the next day I received a phone call from a young lady that I have not spoken to in 14 years. She once lived in the city that I had moved to, New Haven, and I was speaking at an event a year ago, and by revelation, it was revealed that she needed to run for her life. She had really been through turmoil and she needed to make a decision. Two years ago, everything came crashing down. What looked like to be the end really was her beginning, to receive what she was born to do. Reflecting back 15 years ago, it was the promise that God made to her. Things began to change into the "Good Success" that had always been intended for her. She has now recorded albums, books, has her own store in one of the biggest malls in South Carolina and, now, a line of shoes. "Good Success" stepped into it.

As I was pondering one day, meditating on "Good Success" and the plan for the tour to help women all over the world, I started thinking back to over twenty-five years ago when the vision first came. The dream of all of this, the capacity God gave to me when my dear friend and I were flying on a plane to India in 2001. It was our first time to ever have flown that far across the ocean. I knew that He was preparing us to expand our borders, so I began to concentrate and meditate on allowing God to direct me on how to begin to start developing the direction to spearhead the vision. It was 2005, when I began to take the deposit of the vision. I picked up a pen and paper. The more I travelled internationally the more I understood the marketplace from a Global perspective, and I could receive more from God. As more revelations came, I started going back and forth to the Middle East. What I saw in a dream and a vision became a reality. People that were destined to be in my life started showing up and were no longer in the shadows, but made manifest. So my words to all of my readers are for you to measure your personal success to what you were born to do on the earth realm, and do it. It doesn't matter how far away it seems. When you begin to have a purpose and think about your vision and legacy that will last, you will have "Good Success"

CHAPTER 1

Insights—The Origin of Every
Good Achievement

CHAPTER 1

Insights—The Origin of Every Good Achievement

⁴ So, my very dear friends don't get thrown off course. Every desirable and beneficial gift comes out of heaven. The gifts are rivers of light cascading down from the Father of Light. There is nothing deceitful in God, nothing two-faced, nothing fickle. He brought us to life using the true Word, showing us off as the crown of all his creatures.

Current Capacity

Successes and Failures

⁵ Don't give up, you can do it. When you have come through the time of testing, turn to your companions and give them a fresh start"

OVER THE YEARS, I have been exposed to countless people who describe the challenges they face and the obstacles that stand in their way. Most can be categorized, in my mind, as 1) Fear of the unknown, 2) lack of information on the subject, or 3) the painful memory of a past experience. All of these represent real obstacles to the individual that ultimately keep them from achieving God's desired state of abundance in every way in their lives. Kept alive on the inside, they represent the limits of our potential and boundary that stifle the very incredible gift that God has promised us; to open the windows of heaven (the connection with his energy of insight and directions for our lives). However big or small the obstacle is, God has promised that a way of escape has already been designed and put in place for us. Our ability to see these solutions come from our ability to reframe our circumstances, or how we view the obstacles, to allow God to legally work in this realm. Remember that he has given us charge over every small or large thing on the earth and that we have dominion or rule over it. Let's look at how some of the people that I know have reframed their words and worlds to get back on track to greatness.

Fear of the Unknown

It is not uncommon for us to fear the unknown. In fact, most people would rather avoid any changes to the current state given no real reason for change. I emphasize real reason because this life journey is all about the realities that we create. Take for instance the major accomplishments or our forefathers. A local news channel recently reported some predictions made in 1931 of 2011 and what it would be like to live then. One of these was that the [6]"magic of remote control" would be common place" (reference CNN Josh Levs reports. http://www.cnn.com/video/#/video/us/2010/12/19/levs.nyt.predictions. cnn). To the person living in 1931, remote c control technology that we know today would seem a little frightening; as we see it applied in almost every industry (robotics, aerospace, automotive, medical, et.al.). But, we must understand that our ideas are not just for us, they are for the advancement of humanity.

Avoid Calamity

Not all of the behaviors are positive and productive for us. We all probably know of people that engage in negative behaviors that refuse to stop. They become so engaged in the activity (pornography, smoking, drugs) that changing from this activity represents a new person, and unfamiliar territory. [7]"Whoever sows sin reaps weeds, and bullying anger sputters into nothing". The warnings that God gives is provided in sufficient time for us to make the necessary course corrections and avoid calamity. He is such a loving God, that he gives us time to correct these errors in judgment. Even so, I find it difficult to deliver a message of warning from him to a person and for them to receive it and change. It is as if the behavior is something interconnected into the individual themselves.

Legal Papers

I recall this one gentleman that when I met him one day walked into the community facility, Center YMCA, with sharp pains in my stomach, I started praying, asking God what was hidden, I knew that what I was experiencing was not natural and I just prayed and ask god to reveal the plot. Then it became clearer. I had an open vision of phone numbers, papers all flew in the air, and I saw a paper trail, investigation, and I was showed people possibly being jailed. I spoke out what I saw to the gentlemen that I came with to visit. I warned them of what was getting ready to take place so that they wouldn't get caught in the snare that came to strangle their destiny. You are meant to have Good Success!

Funeral Home—Investigations

A decade ago a really good friend of mine worked for a large television company in New York City but lived in Connecticut and he asked me if I knew anyone that owned a funeral home in the city because he was making a movie and needed to get some footage for his film. I said "Yes, my cousin was married to a man who owns one, I will ask her". Well the opportunity came up when my God sister died, and I had to go to the funeral home for my God mother. When I got to the funeral home, I told my cousin about the opportunity that my friend had presented about filming a movie. I said "Hey cousin, I have a friend who wants to make a movie, and he wanted to know can he use the facility and that he would pay for the facility". Well, her husband went crazy when she asked about the movie right in front of me, she was so embarrassed. I felt really bad for her, but more than that, I was able to see right through that whole ordeal. I prayed right on the spot and asked God what was really the problem and the answers that came to me were unbelievable. Without tangible facts, people would just think that one would be crazy or something is wrong. I left telling my friend what had happened. I said he is hiding something; he doesn't want anyone to know. I took a good look at the set-up of my surroundings and I wanted to run real fast out of that place and prayed that my cousin would get free. If I had never had to go there, I would have never known that a movie was taken place already. The authorities came in a month later and dug up bodies of people's family members who had been lying in the basement in body bags that were never properly buried. If you compromise and start operating in fear you will never have "Good Success" that is intended for you.

Those individuals who find themselves in a place of fear from taking the sufficient steps toward implementing the creative insights that God has given them, I would recommend that they first find a way to work or volunteer in the profession that they are interested in. Believe in yourself and work for knowledge. Gain the necessary skills and backing needed to gain more confidence and faith.

Knowledge is power

Learn from the greatest in your field, and stay in contact with them. Find an expert and follow what they are doing. Be proactive about your future and try to do something no matter how small every single day.

For those who find themselves addicted to or trapped in the spiraling cycle of unhealthy behaviors, know that there are consequences to every action. Continually engaging in this activity opens the door to more and unhealthier behaviors and the spirit world that supports it.

Painful memories are not true indication of future results.

Most of us can recall a time or two where we experienced some painful memories and vowed never to repeat or allow us to experience that again. When we are wounded, scar tissue is formed and becomes a sober reminder of the experience. These wounds are relationship, financial losses, accidents, hereditary, and others. All of these leave painful memories. There was one lady that I knew decided to change her religion because of the pain she endured from her husband who professed to be a Christian. There are countless other stories I could offer here, but the fact remains, each painful memory seems to take up its own corner of our memories waiting for us to encounter a similar circumstance to remind us of how we failed before.

So in each case, we tend to latch onto the circumstance and its makeup and decide how we will interpret the future based on that experience. Our mind is then held by the limits that are placed on it. "I have been down that road before," or "every person from that race is a certain way." We seem to hold onto the very thing that keeps us down.

⁸ It happens so regularly that it's predictable. The moment I decide to do good, evil is there to trip me up. I truly delight in God's commands, but it's pretty obvious that not all of me join in that delight. Parts of me covertly rebel, and just when I least expect it, they take charge.

Here, we also struggle with the things of the past and the pleasures of the body from doing the perfect will of God and achieving greatness. This warring goes on in our mind. Renew it. Restore and replace it with the creative words of God, "LET THERE BE . . ."

God reminds us of the struggles with creating as it plays out with the story of mankind itself. He created us, and said that it was good. He was pleased with his creation. It pained him to have to discuss this with men from times past, even in the garden and he separated himself from his creation. Even then, God saw his and man's future together and began to work on it. In this example the scars of time and relationship separated man from his creator. But God knew the potential that he had created. He knows how to provide the balance in our lives for us to know how good He is to us. He continues to reveal the future to us and who He intends us to be.

But most important about failures is the valuable lessons learned. A child that begins to walk sometimes falls, but regains their balance and tries again. For example, Bill Gates grabs his boot straps after being turned down by IBM; Thomas Edison discovers hundreds of ways not to design a light bulb; The small business owner challenged to compete against the large chain, creatively learns how to brand themselves with a personal touch; The neighborhood church that finds its community demographics changed and adjusts to become more diverse in its presentation of God. All of these are insights that are learned from the challenge of a failure or the challenges we face with change. Let each of your failures be teaching moments and watch as fewer and fewer failures appear at your door.

CHAPTER 2

Moving and Developing
the Ideas and Insights

CHAPTER 2

Moving and Developing the Ideas and Insights

Innovations—Struggles are Opportunities— The breeding ground for new ideas

[9] *Because of the extravagance of those revelations, and so I wouldn't get a big head, I was given the gift of a handicap to keep me in constant touch with my limitations. Satan's angel did his best to get me down; what he in fact did was push me to my knees. No danger then of walking around high and mighty! At first I didn't think of it as a gift, and begged God to remove it. Three times I did that, and then he told me,*

My grace is enough; it's all you need. My strength comes into its own in your weakness.

[10] *Once I heard that, I was glad to let it happen. I quit focusing on the handicap and began appreciating the gift. It was a case of Christ's strength moving in on my weakness. Now I take limitations in stride, and with good cheer, these limitations that cut me down to size—abuse, accidents, opposition, bad breaks. I just let Christ take over! And so the weaker I get, the stronger I become.*

MAN IS ENDOWED with the greatest gift: choice. We are allowed to choose the paths that we take and have the ability to change direction and course as necessary. We can choose to be rich, live healthy, or with an abundance of peace. I am reminded of past generations who experienced severe economic times and struggles. I often ask seniors what was their most memorable rocking chair memory. You may be surprised with some of the responses, but I ask you to imagine yourself in a place of retirement transition. What does this look like to you? If this is difficult for you to imagine, choose today to start painting a vivid picture of what that looks like. Are you healthy, vibrant, and able to teach others? Do you see yourself exploring the corners of the Earth that few have seen? That path to this picture, the new reality, may need some time and thought, but the next path to getting there is filled with possibilities. This I refer to as innovations of insight.

I recall one very bright engineer's story to me years ago, who called me to describe a near miss auto accident. He was stopped behind a car at a traffic light. ". . . As I began to accelerate from a stopped position, I was distracted by something to my right that took my eyes off the road in front of me. Before I knew it, the car in front of me stopped for some reason. When I looked up, I immediately applied my brakes and avoided a rear-end collision." I asked him what did he get out of the incident, and probed a little at the near miss that happened to him. He replied, "You know, if I really think about it, my car should have known that it was approaching the car in front of me and applied the brakes, or warning light, as a result. It is not a stretch of the imagination that a simple software code could be designed and implemented for this fix. It would be to the advantage of insurance companies and car owners alike for this innovation to be put in new vehicles." So I reminded him that he should take action right away on the innovation that was imputed into his mind and try to research patents for the concept. He waited, and took no action. Years later, he called me again and said, "I am so sorry that I did not listen to you. You know the design software fix that we talked about years ago; I just saw a commercial on the television where the fix has been implemented on new premium cars. I could just shoot myself in the foot."

Innovations are all around us today. God has not only given us the choice to experience good and bad events, but He has also given us the ability to continually improve on our current environment to make life better for us. The world needs our innovative abilities to continue to bring new products and services to the market. So think for a minute, what bad experience that you had to endure either through your striving for a better life, something that was inherited to you through past generations, or thrust upon you by sheer accident? Regardless of the incident, innovative solutions are there for us to create the future we desire. It just takes a little coaching and thought, and you will be well on your way to achieving "Good Success".

For every action, there is an equal and opposite reaction. Jets overcome gravity, and angels overcome demons.

Angels and Demons

"Good Success" is for good and not evil. I learned that first hand after being on the front line of a real live fight, not read or heard about, but dead smack in the middle of what some might call spiritual warfare. I knew that the way that I was coming out, was going to determine how I was going to help others when they went through their own war. It was one of the most difficult things in life that I had to experience. When I was thrust into this battle, I knew before I entered the battle, why, how, and what the outcome would be, so I knew it was for "Good Success", and not evil. What I could not control was the different processes but I knew it was the price of life I had to embrace for the first time.

If you let the truth be told, it did not feel good, because I did not have control. I tried to avoid the ordeal by reasoning with officials after the event took place, but the delegated authority did not want to listen. I did not want this story to take the course it was heading due to embarrassment I had foreseen. However, I now understand because of all of the similar events that have happen in the United States Judicial System this process had to run its course for as long as it did, because the authorities that were involved would not look into the matter nor do an internal investigation. I took a plane to Savannah, Georgia and stayed two weeks to try and meet with the authorities that were involved to give them a warning before this two-year plus ordeal took place. In 1998, I began a real life story of the American university education system with official police officers who had no integrity as well as the higher level authorities in the American judicial court system. The master plan of criminal justice 101 began and I saw "Good Success". One early morning, I was awakened by a dream from heaven that was given to me by God. Understand that God will always give you "Good Success". Whether you know him or not, he rains on the just as well as the unjust. It's good to know that you will always have sweet and bitter, night and day, and angels and demons. At the end of the day when you do right, "Good Success" will always come to you. I woke up after the messenger came to me in my dream and visitation to let me know that the demons were plotting to set my son up and frame him. It was all I could do to help him fight that he was innocent and that the almighty King would uncover the lie.

I woke up and entered back into my natural state which is man. I sat up in the middle of my bed and said, "What is this? What are you talking about God?" Like any mother, you call your child. I picked up the phone to call him while he was away at college in Savannah State University in Savannah, Georgia. It was the early morning hour. I called and woke him up. He was sleeping but I made him talk with me for a while, until I was sure I had a feel for what was going on. He had an early class that morning and wanted to go back to sleep, but moms all over the world know how to find out information from their children. So, I released him after a long while, and I couldn't go back to sleep. I just continued to meditate, pray and study while I waited for the outcome of the dream earlier that morning. Well, later that morning, around the 8:00 hour my phone rang, and it was a lady's voice on the other end saying. "This is Mrs. Doe calling from Savannah State University Police Department. Your son screamed out your number, and said "Mam, please call my mother", and she said I don't know what Mr. Wilcox is doing to these boys but he just brought them in hand cuffs." I said, "May I speak to the officer please". Mr. Wilcox got on the phone and acknowledged who he was, and said to me, "Are you Ms. Wearing?" I said, "Yes." He said, "I am bringing your son, Mr. Wearing, in for some questioning. He will be released, shortly, but we will hold him until we are finished." So, I asked what was going on and what happened?" and he replied "That he couldn't tell me anything right now, but he wanted to ask me if I had been talking to my son earlier that morning," and I said, "Yes." He said, "What time was that?" and that was when I heard the Spirit of god say "Don't tell him anything to feed him information because he was one of the ones trying to set the plot". My heart dropped in the middle of my stomach, and the Holy Spirit said to tell him this, "You better be very careful of what plot you are trying to set for Wearing because when you do things to others to try and destroy them, you know that the eyes of God are everywhere, and He sees everything. He will overthrow that which is being set up. So, Sir, I hope you have a fear of God." Mr. Wilcox then said that his father was a preacher, and I said, "There are a lot of preachers, and I hope he is righteous and taught you to be upright, because within six months you will be found out." Forty-eight hours into the process, my son was then transferred to the town jail house in Savannah, Georgia. I called back, the lady on the phone said "Mam, I don't know why Mr. Wilcox is doing what he is doing, but he is the only cop, on the case." I knew then I needed to get to town, and also warn the other college officials and put them on notice. I showed up early Monday morning unexpectedly on a journey that I did not want to go on but had to, knowing my endeavors would end in "Good Success".

This is part of my first-hand account of dealing with angels and demons my journey to "Good Success". You must read the full story in my upcoming book of this true story. The full newspaper article can be found at this web address:

http://savannahnow.com/stories/100900/LOCssuarrests.shtml

Developing your insights

You may be in a place where things have not been the best for you or the timing may not be convenient for you. But if you press forward and follow that insight or idea you have been developing in your heart or mind this is your greatest hour. It is time for you to have Good Success.

Let me take the time and walk you through two weeks of Good Success Habits. You must have a made up mind that you are going to be successful so that you can accomplish your vision and the Legacy you are about to lay or build upon. Declare that you will (I will) complete this new foundation that I am getting ready to start and finish, wherever I am in the world or whatever I am going to develop, "I WILL" have the tenacity to finish what I am going to develop.

Strokes of Genius

Strokes of genius are those witty ideas you have or get of an innovation or invention, that comes out of a creative mode. It is when you get an idea of something that has not been done before, or something that has been created but you come up with another dimension of a better version, or enhance what already is in existence, and is the next phase of the product and solutions.

Strokes of genius are great when you can come up with tangible ideas that can be produced into a tangible product. There are many things, like concepts, solutions you may have, even theory you can go to the market with, or a product to sell or try. You are walking in a different dimension now because you can package for trade in a global market. That can cause you to create a demand and also have supply that will cause you to have great and "Good Success". It makes it all better when you start a standard that benefits humanity from the stroke of genius ideas that are not harmful or destructive by going along to leave legacies in the world.

Strokes of genius people benefit from moving forward on the genius ideas. They are the real genius. You who are not smart keep ideas inside your head, or some say in your heart. What good is it doing in there? The people that begin to move forward with their ideas and not wonder what will happen, but will make it happen, are the real geniuses. Once you have developed your plan, put it into action experience the real demonstration of having a stroke of genius idea, you are well on your way to having "Good Success". Don't have an idea, do nothing about it, and you will watch it on television years later having missed out on "Good Success".

When mysteries are being real to you by dreams or visions, who will ever know if it is going to take you somewhere, if you don't try? Don't wait to have an "I wish or I should have" experience.

The Little Man

My husband and I met in what was orchestrated by God. His arrival and my desire to stand fast on the promises of God yielded great benefits. After just deciding to spend some time together, I introduced him to my mentor that was visiting the area. During the meeting, while the three of us were riding in the car he replied ". . . what is this flame that I see between you, . . . this is more than a business relationship . . . who is this little boy that I see . . ." Confirmation of this little boy came from a praying mother, during a later conversation without a physical meeting. We discuss more details during or discussion on the art of listening, but safe to say, the little man (son) did arrive.

This real life mystery of visions and dreams:

My miracle of Good Success son is almost three and he is a real little genius, his Dr. told us when he was six months that he was going to be unique and smart, well he started recognizing his name on Bill Boards and Marke at nine months, and counting money out of the cash register in front of a client of mine who happen to be a child psych, Dr. L jumps out of chair that she was sitting in, and goes over to the counter to see with her own eyes, because she could hear him but couldn't see him, I had to see that because had you told me that I would have never believed you she said! He is also reading short stories, recognizing words, and working math solutions with his dad, but has a memory of old, sings all the patriotic songs, and is learning the piano.

Inheritance

Inheritance is very important in everyone's life. A good upright man will leave something for the generation to come and will have a plan for them, after he has departed from the earth. I was having a family conversation with my aunt, my grandmother's eldest child, Mae Donna, and we were sharing about how my, and her father, and his father left a beautiful inheritance to their generation for the next generation that whoever will be born in the family would never have to worry about land or somewhere to stay. Even if you have many in the family, you will always have that as part of the inheritance of being a part of the family. Our forefathers where not filled with degrees, but were very smart. Back in those times, they knew how to keep the inheritance in the family. They had a stroke of genius moment when the elders got together and masterminded for the family, whom they would never see, but knew would come. They put it in black and white; made it there in ink so that it could never be amended. Our inheritance will never be divided in divorce or even be split in disagreement.

Our inheritance is the ceiling from where each of us, if we take the opportunity, can launch from to an even better place. This is why you should start thinking about your legacies that you want and need to leave. This is not a selfish act. You must begin to not only help where you are in your life by working for someone else, but what are you going to do for yourself. I challenge you to look at your life today and ask the question, "When am I going to take the responsibility of developing and stop blaming someone else for not succeeding and change my own mind and situation?" Take responsibility and leave a legacy.

Focus

Focus to me is a big word for this book "Good Success, Visions and Legacies That Last". What my grandmother said to me three weeks before she went to sleep, was focus on what you are supposed to do on this earth. It changed my life forever, and caused me to complete the seventeen books that I had to write. Her words were [13]"focus on yourself and don't worry about what anyone else is doing" standing next to her bedside along with my uncle and cousin. I said "Shush! Shush!" She is speaking for our family, be quiet and let's receive what she wants to leave us. So I decided to take that word "focus" and run for my life, and complete what I know. It meant I was helping a whole lot of people to do their vision, but it was time for me to now focus and be accountable for what I needed to do on this earth. I had to focus on what I was born to do. So part of the "Good Success" book, Focus, and all of this above had started over two decades ago, but it was not time for it to come full speed ahead. I knew I was faithful in helping others, but now was the time and season to focus.

Persistence, a necessary ingredient for "Good Success"

Persistence is a necessary ingredient for "Good Success". If you are not persistent and diligent like when you are getting paid to do someone else's payroll, you will not succeed. Ask yourself if your company closed down today or had to go through what is called right siding for the benefit of the future forecast of the company, or you just got fired or was lay off for poor performance, what would you do? Well, today I want to say to you, you must be persistent for yourself, like when you had to show up for someone else's vision for your employment. So put aside some time to plan, your vision legacy that you have to leave on the earth. Just remember that how you are for someone else will be the performance that will be due back to you.

From Work to Passion

Find something you like doing and you will become wealthy. If you are doing something you dread doing, you will not have a good rate on your return nor are you benefiting someone else that is employing you. Some people are swift to resort to passions.

I have seen and watched so many people from different walks of life complain about the kind of work they are presently in or made comments about what their boss or company should be doing and I would comment, where is your vision or company so that you can do what you want or think should be done.

When you become the boss then you can make an executive decision. I have seen companies fold up and go under. People want to complain that their time was up, and they have funded their course. If you had time in, you would have or should have been ready to start your own company like you were working at. That is if you loved what you were doing for work and it was a passion. If you are somewhere that you can't stand working or it can't take you to a better place or further you, then you are wasting other people's time and, more importantly, your own. You don't value yourself. So find something you love doing and it will cause you to become wealthy

[14] *"Find something you love to do, and you'll never work a day in your life"*
—*Harvey MacKay*

Passion that endures the test of time

Passion will always endure the test of time because you are more passionate about what you're doing and you value it. You will not easily give up when you are passionate about what you are involved in. Sometimes situations come up expected and unexpected, but when you love what you are doing, it will endure the test of time. You will find ways to make it work and are willing to do what is right to keep it working because you believe in it.

Supply and Demand

Supply and demand is if you find a need for something there will be a demand for it. It could be something like you want an iPad. You and the whole world know it is a demand. We can ask ourselves the question what did you do before you had one? You made it work, right? But, now that you have one, you don't understand how you got along without it.

Timing and Seasons: There's a Right Time for Everything

[15] "There is a right time for everything. There is an opportune time to do things for everything on the earth." I am in my forties and when I was in my high school back in 1981, they were talking about the jobs that would be obsolete twenty or thirty years from then and how the technology and innovation would be the grid that would change the world with a global economy along with personal and medical services etc. Technology as we know it would continue to have a market in our future. When you talk about Steve Jobs leaving an awesome legacy on the earth, it is a good evaluation of the right time for everything.

Old Wells and New wells

Let's not quarrel, be jealous of or beat down the wealth of others (these are considered old wells). Do not presume that all those who possess wealth are greedy or stake claim to riches that are not ours. Let us instead seek wise counsel from those who have prospered before us and left legacies to be built on or patterned after. Those persons or businesses can become partners or stakeholders to help build your idea (these are new wells).

As an example, WGEC is helping, training and mentoring women globally to develop their ideas who have not gone to market to become successful. We are inviting persons who are and have been walking in Good Success to partner with us. We welcome entrepreneurs, women in business, and business professionals who are experts in the fields of marketing, finances, technology, business development, branding, patents, research, international business, community development, etc. to mentor women across the global marketplace via our virtual Women's Entrepreneur Global Center. We have women that own several different franchises as well as women who are legal professionals, entrepreneurs, and experts in economics and much more mentoring at our center.

Listen, it doesn't matter who has a similar idea, just mind your own business on where to start digging your new well. Be innovative and set down your intentions of where you are going to start your digging, if you worry about others you will never have a place to drink from fresh living waters. Seize the opportunity and value the time you have on earth to leave a legacy.

Improving on an old idea

Improving an old idea you must know if you can take it somewhere on the technology grid or if it still has life in the living organism or has it run its course. In the last decade, companies across the globe have had to re-evaluate the jobs of the organization. Some had to be shut down, but some had room to improve the old ideas, or branch off. They became the new innovators with old ideas proving the test of time with new energy.

Prophetic Insights

Prophetic insight belongs to people with vision. If you have people around you who still have not had a revelation for themselves, then some things are just passed away. They are caught up in things from yester years and don't realize it's not working for them. They are outdated and don't have vision, It's like old wine and new wine it doesn't mix. You can appear to still look like what you are still participating in is working, but because of the outcome you know it's time to shift. However, you are so full of you, it's hard to let go of what was, because of what appears to be working. But, you don't have growth unless you let go. The reality is you need to go over your vision plan for today in this 21st century and make plans for the future. Sometimes leaders need to get into a mode of mentoring and become teachers while they still have strength to impart and pass the torch while it has fire. If you still can't forecast your growth from quarter to quarter, from year to year, then you are not having "Good Success" versus just merely existing. You must have insight into what, where, who, and how, and when to get to where you want to go. This is the hour that as leaders, you should want to align yourself with strong people around you who are also leaders, that are gold medalist. Leaders take notes to your surroundings when your inner circle won't let other talented people connect with you or try and destroy others individual character. Learn how to study people from all walks of life and don't let others define people for you. Make time to get to know individuals even if you have to study them from a far. You must have prophetic insight to know who is supposed to be connected to you.

CHAPTER 3

Getting Expert Help

CHAPTER 3

Getting Expert Help

The Heart Attack

I HAD A speaking engagement. I call it a divine assignment or engagement from God. I was called into this city where I was born as a child to speak to a group of people. I knew part of my assignment before I got there, but did not have the full picture of what was going to supernaturally happen that night to all of the people. Well, the one thing that was revealed to me before I got to this particular event was that while we are living here on the earthly realm, we have the power that has been given to us to create our God given assignment with purpose so that we may have "Good Success". I spoke that there is more for you here than you are reaching. God wants you to live to fulfill why you were born, not only live, but to live in good health even as your soul prospers, you are to prosper overall.

I began to pray. Immediately, I saw an open vision of a heart that entered into the doors, like a super human-sized person, but it was a heart, and I knew that I had come for the purpose to speak and change the direction of the life of all people in the audience that day, so that they have "Good Success". I understood that success comes in different forms and ways to individual lives. I then said to the audience of people, there are some of you that have physical conditions here, and there is a miracle from heaven to those that receive this miracle, so that you may live and not die, but have long life. A few people moved out to get prayed for, but I felt a grievance spirit come into the room and, then, the heart went straight to my back. I turned around and saw that it was the leader standing behind me, and I shouted, "Oh, it is you." He tried to deny the truth and did not receive it. He actually dismissed it religiously and went into a place of denial. I then saw into the future, of the outcome of the matter. I prayed for the wife of the leader. I didn't know all of what was going to be left for her to carry out. I followed the instructions of the Lord, and prayed strength to you. It was up to God to establish her with what he had equipped her for and give her all the resources that she was going to need to carry on the great commission so that she would have "Good Success". Two months later to the date, the husband died of a massive heart attack and the funeral service took place as I had seen. That night, I received a phone call, asking could I come to speak the next morning at the service of worship. Well, I did and God opened up a vision again once I got there and exposed a man that would come to try and take over. This was a businessman that had died, and a community leader that had his legacies laid in place, so that men with ungodly motives on a mission were working out of order. It was in the heart of this wicked man that it was revealed. The man was buried on Friday, and I was called in to speak Sunday. It was the following week the man showed up to deliver the message what he said was God, he wanted to take over and be in charge not knowing God had said no in advance. The wife told him, "we were expecting you to come because God had revealed the way you would come in, now get out".

Isn't it awesome, that wicked hearts of people are revealed, and when you are around the right person in your life that has the gift of God, he will always expose the plan of the betrayer, so that you have "Good Success"? Not that "Good Success" won't come, but evil won't overtake you if you listen.

Mentoring

Mentoring is important to get in your journey and when you get the right mentor, you will see the importance of repeating the "Good Success" of your mentor. If you don't have a mentor, and you need one, find someone in the area of expertise of what you are trying to accomplish. If it is a business then you want someone who has traveled that road and is now successful and who is ready to teach and instruct.

What I've learned over the years is that if someone crosses my path more than once asking the same advice God did not assign them to me. That person has taken my valued time for free. As a mentor I only sow into fallow ground so that those who listen will reap the benefits and prosper others.

My track record is that everyone who has followed my instruction has had Good Success. If God has assigned me to you then you value your instructor and you will have good success. There will be people out there who do not heed this message and they may find themselves in the same place they were in before they read this book. Often times people seek advice when God has already shown them the answer, but when God gives you the tools all you have to do is use them. Ask yourself what are you an expert in and then can it be packaged into a reproducible product. My challenge to you as a mentor is to heed the advice given to in this book and you will have good success.

I've known people for over twenty years and they don't take heed to my advice and they are still in the same place. Over the past two years I have been mentoring a young woman who desired to adopt. I explained to her that she needed to get her home ready and prepare for her child. She began the process and fulfilled all legal requirements and waited on God. She and her husband planned their long awaited honeymoon after seven years of marriage. At the eleventh hour before they were scheduled to leave I received a phone call. The adoption agency was looking for a family for a newborn baby boy. Within six days they became the proud parents of a baby boy. All because they followed instructions and got prepared.

There are a lot of people who can be mentors and have lot of wisdom on this earth to impart to you g people. Young people should be able to live vicariously through them and learn from their mistakes. I am calling on the future mentors to rise up and impart knowledge where there is need and leave a legacy that will last. There a segment of people who attain knowledge and keep it for themselves they do not allow other people to live vicariously through them and learn from their mistakes. So, successful people join us in our endeavor mentoring other women worldwide to stimulate the economy and benefit humanity.

Role Models

Role models are representatives that are good images of the model of what you want to be when you grow up and help you to advance in life. They are clear images. This is a close-up angel. You can desire to be like someone from afar, but you need a role model that you have access to. The role model needs to have time for you and you need to be ready to listen and be mentored.

Shadowing

Shadowing is when you can look at someone, but see yourself. Even when you and others see you, people will begin to say "you remind me of . . . ," and it's a positive statement. A learned behavior of success is a good one, because you can learn vicariously when you shadow someone. If you pay attention, you can do better than your shadow because you can learn from all of their mistakes.

Increasing Your Faith (Eliminating Fears)

Increasing your faith and eliminating your fears will get you to where you would like to go. That's when you look up and wonder how you got there. When you really increase your faith, you will come to understand that it was supernatural all along. It's like the faith of starting a race and your end is the finish line. Before you know it, you are the Gold Medalist. Increasing your faith helps when you prepare for the race, or journey, and all fear is gone.

Contract and Legal Protection

Contract and legal protection is the most important step. It makes sure everyone, you and contributing parties, are covered. Everyone has a clear understanding so that there are no misunderstandings. Start out by having contracts in place. Enter into not only a verbal but written understanding for "Good Success". I meet wonderful people all of the time, and want to do business with them. However make sure the relationship is protected with written understanding, the integrity of how you do business with other people and cultures is vital, in today's Global Marketplace.

CHAPTER 4

Dawn of a New Day

CHAPTER 4

Dawn of a New Day

A Dark Place

ONE SUNDAY AFTERNOON, I was between services. At the time, my commute to church was about an hour's drive but I wanted to return to the evening service. I didn't have any assignment anywhere else. But on this particular Monday afternoon, I was leaving the driveway of the church after 12:00 noon prayer time and I received a 911 mandated assignment to go to. I would be visited by a man that would come up to me, and try to flirt with me because of the way I looked. Well, after I got there, I had a late lunch. I sat there meditating while I was eating. I had my head down relaxing when the door to the restaurant opened and closed with a loud slam. I immediately looked up and I felt something that I could not describe at that time. My intuition said, "That is him, and he will come up to you". He did and began to say how beautiful I was. I said thank you. I then received and was bid to tell him to come out of that dark place that he was presently in, because in that dark place there was no plan for God in his life. "God said he comes that you have "Good Success", but if you don't come out of that dark place, you will be in a place of utter darkness where you can't see. Sir, it doesn't matter if I ever see you again, I am trying to help you before you get to the end of this thing that you are wrestling with." The man then said, "Oh boy, I ran into one of those church people again, like my family, telling me what God said. Let me get out of here". I reminded him that he came to me trying to flirt. I said "Good day and I hope you listen, sir. Your life has to be important, because I was mandated to come to this place today and wait for you to come and approach me."

Five years later, my sister moved into her new apartment and was hosting a Thanksgiving feast at her house and invited close friends over to give thanks. She had everyone who did not have friends or family gather at her house. Well, some of her friends invited their family members along with them and they all began to come up the stairs. I saw a man come up and he happened to be blind. I didn't say anything. Everyone got together to pray before we started eating. I was asked to pray, and as I started talking, the man started crying, saying "Oh my God, Oh my God. It is God's servant, it's her. It's her." Everyone asked what he was talking about. He then said remember I told you about this woman that came to warn me about what was going to happen to me if I did not change my ways, and to come out of that dark place, or that I would find myself in a place of utter darkness. Well this is the result. I am blind because I did not listen. My God, I prayed that I would run into you again. I did not know where or how. My God, I will never forget your voice, I wish I had listened. I am praying that I can see again and I have changed my life. I now understand that you came because God wanted "Good Success" for me. I had a choice and I made the wrong one. The blind man said, "People listen to me when I say that she said when the Lord says something just listen. I testify wherever I go.

Anticipating the "New" Arrival

Anticipating the New Arrival is like when you are pregnant, waiting on a very important package or good news that awaits you. Anything that gets you excited. When you're laying a foundation of your new vision, business plan, you must have this same anticipation about your new investment. Set your stage so that when the curtain goes up, you are anticipating the new arrival that you just gave birth to.

Building and supporting networks

You must know that building and supporting networks are important to your success and take you farther than your money. It is the key to success that money can't purchase. Relationships are very important so make sure you make note of every introduction. You just never know how far that water is flowing.

Prepare for Stretching

Make sure you are physically in shape because you will be stretched in more ways than one. You will find yourself making decisions that you did not anticipate. You will move out of your comfort zone. If you find yourself being moved put, laid off, or "right-sided" create your own exit strategy. Make your vision come to life and create your own business and support your own workforce.

From Your Job to Work

Your job you have little responsibility in the big picture. It provides training ground that God has given you to perfect your skill. As an example, a shepherd boy that turns into a great leader of people provides a clear illustration of how what you work at daily prepares you for God's work. To get to the next place in God, consider his work for you, and begin to own the power that He has given you. When I have to make a decision or declaration, I change my own mind, from the way I am presently going. I start to rethink where you want to be, and lay strategies to how you are going to get there. Your job, in the job mind set, is something you feel that you have to do in order to meet your present needs, but it does not touch the real truth about God's life work for you. Work speaks about, I am working and I have to do well, in order to get the next promotion. In work, you really have to work hard to accomplish things. So, you mind set is totally different. You even handle work in a delicate way, as if it where your own because if you don't excel, you can't and won't get the desires and sense of accomplishment.

At work you have more responsibility. Yes, it involves a more in depth understanding pressure and stress more than what on the surface. It involves changing your mind to understand the opportunities and every adverse circumstance it brings. To understand this more, I would like to offer the following three strategies on the new you, your new normal that breaks the dawn of the new day you are heading into. First, anticipate the new arrival. Second, Prepare by building your supporting networks. Third, prepare for the work, prepare for the stretching.

This is how work can take you into owning your own business if that is your desire or passion. You have to work smart and be prepared to launch yourself into the Dawn of a New Day. Start by considering what you do now, wherever you do it, and whenever you do it. You have to work hard at it, if you work it, it will work. Get smarter that you are now on how this job and work is going to fill a demand. Today is a perfect day to get started if you are reading this book, I challenge you to start today by having a conscious thought. If you are already thinking of it, you can make it happen. It all starts with conception and remembering whatever you do for someone else that will be the measure that is given back to you. When you are at a job, you are at someone else's business. But when you are at work, you have destiny and legacies on your mind. Be a good shepherd while you are at your job, and consider how those daily, seemingly meaningless tasks, are preparing you for your legacy. You may not become a competitor, but you will begin to shape the very direction for you and your family. Learn even more that what you need to learn, and define what it is you may want to embark upon.

So start by one day, seeing your own employees, and envision how you would when you own workers to become. How would you teach them about work, to be a model to move to the top of the food chain, to out the door among your own business. Consider that a smarter employee is able to help you reach your own goals more efficiently.

Project: Technology, Innovations, and Green/Renewable Energy (TIGRE)

The U.S. has to find new ways to rebuild its workforce. While the country is still the world's strongest economy, the competitive edge is eroding. There is a growing concern among business leaders that the ability to find good workers with the right skills and abilities to meet talent needs will be impossible[1]. This situation is intensified given the existing academic achievement gap and levels of poverty resulting in an underutilized labor market. The goal of a TIGRE-type project is to help strengthen the local labor pool through delivery of rigorous supplemental learning programs targeted at disadvantaged youth grades 8th through 12 (13 to 18 years of age). Why this age group? There are a number of reasons to be discussed later, but this group represents the new-entry work force in the very near future and is in positions to receive that highest payback on training and educational initiatives. While, building fundamental skills earlier in a child's academic experience is preferable, the emphasis of the TIGRE Project is building a more immediate pipeline of diverse talent for businesses to leverage.

---

[1] Reference notes 1)

The TIGRE Project is conceived in recognition of the fact that innovations in technology, science, engineering and new energy sources will be areas for future job growth. The ability for the current and next generation to exhibit strong mathematical, reading, writing, and critical-thinking skills; as well as individual leadership and collaboration will be essential. TIGRE has two primary goals: 1) Build strong human capital assets to enable greater economic success at the individual and community level; 2) Create a reputable pool of talent able to pursue post-secondary education or professional training in the science, technology, engineering, and mathematics (STEM) areas to maintain adequate technology and science related talent pool to meet future employer demands in the nation.

By 2018, with an expected return to healthy economic growth, but no change in current labor force participation rates or immigration rates, there will likely be more jobs than people to fill them. Some of the technical jobs requirements will be filled with global outsourcing. However, that will not fill the demand. In addition, if the baby boom generation retires from the labor force at the same rate and age as current older workers, the generation that follows will likely be too small to fill many of the projected new jobs. There could be at least 5 million potential job vacancies in the U. S., nearly half of them (2.4 million) in social sector jobs in education, health care, government and nonprofit organizations[2]. All of them requiring talent with fundamental skills and abilities to succeed.

Another key factor for the United States is that African Americans and Hispanics are severely underrepresented in science and engineering, key areas of future job growth. In the future, many of these jobs will be filled by workers from developing countries like China and India[3]. Also, global outsourcing will help fill the demand for labor. However, equipping a greater percentage of the African American and Hispanic population to fully participate in the emerging labor market is important for the US to remain strong.

The TIGRE Project has targeted disadvantage youth, with a special emphasis on the African American and Hispanic population. Different country could uses this same analysis to determine which groups are underrepresented, and offer the best payback on similar type initiatives. This emphasis is based on the fact that the preparedness of this population to participate in the shifting job market is lacking as previously noted. Manufacturing and low skilled jobs have severely declined and new manufacturing jobs will require greater technical savvy and decision making skills. Other areas of job growth are projected to be in areas requiring specialized training or advance education as well. With high percentages of

---

[2] Reference notes 1)
[3] Reference notes 8)

high school dropout rates and incomplete college experiences the unemployment rates for this population will remain some of the highest in the US without intervention. Similar to efforts currently underway in developing nations, it is imperative that the U.S. invest in better preparing members of society to be competitive in the near and long-term job market. It will address the following:

- What are the achievement gaps for students 13 to 18 that stand as impediment to college and professional training
- Evaluate and provide solutions to drop out rate contributing factors
- Cleary define (and update as appropriate) the barriers to college entry, with a targeted 10% (See measurement) improvement in the rate of students attending college after high school, and complete the 4-year degree. This measurement should commensurate with resources available.
- Assessment and evaluation of candidate risk factors that stand as barriers to success.

The TIGRE Project Overview

The vision of the program is to create a new center of excellence, a world leader in the development of a workforce prepared for careers in STEM industries. Like Silicon Valley is to the west, these centers can be developed across different regions. The first phase of the project will target high potential, at risk youth (ages 13-18). Find the most populous municipalities. The 13-18 age range represents a large percentage of its population under the age of 18. The project includes the following objectives:

- **Skills enhancement:** skill building to increase academic performance in math, reading and writing; and professional and leadership development (e.g. planning, prioritizing, teamwork, etc.).
- **Building an appetite for science and technology:** leveraging creative and innovative ways to engage students in pursing science and technology careers; as well as presenting a case for strengthening core skills to prepare for future opportunities.
- **Career exploration and planning:** providing exposure to careers and related job requirements; industries and business concepts to promote knowledge building and

awareness. Focus on jobs that provide economic advancement opportunities (e.g. *Green Energy, Aerospace and Defense, Traffic Engineering, Health Sciences like Nursing Information Science, Business Management of Information Technology Professionals, Entertainment Interactive Designers and Social media, Online Marketing, et. al.*)

• **Parental and community involvement**: implementing approaches that require parent participation and support; designing team projects that provide solutions for local business leaders.

The TIGRE program should:

1. Seek out high potential youth who have limited exposure to college, vocational, or professional skills training initiatives already in place in Connecticut.
2. Implement innovative ways for self discovery; and personal and academic growth.
3. Support individual successes through the Advanced Life Coaching and Career Mentor Matching (ALCCMM) model. Contact me if you are interested, or want to know more about in this program.
4. Create and nurture critical skills for career advancement, and
5. Provide top US companies and small business with access to a targeted pipeline of skilled and talented professionals to meet future labor and employment objectives.

Training Activities

Training activities will align with existing community programs and respond to needs not currently addressed. This will create an integrated workforce development plan. The end result will be one that incorporates short, medium, and long-term planning to meet employers' current and future workforce needs. The plan focuses grant resources from government and private donors into one or more of the following occupations and industries with growth potential:

• **Engineering and Technical—**
   o Aerospace (and related) Engineering fields
   o Traffic Engineering—
      ▪ Solutions to ongoing population growth and technologies (electric car grids and infrastructure)

- Congestions and Roadway SMARTCAR solutions (integration of global positioning systems into re-routing around congested highways)
- High Speed Railway (http://www.america2050.org/2011/12/house-high-speed-rail-hearing-missed-the-point.html)

- **Aerospace and Manufacturing**
  o Lean Manufacturing and Machining Programming and Control
  o Unmanned Vehicles System and Control—The New Pilots

- **Health Sciences**
  o Service and Medical Assisting
  o Nursing Information Science—Data analysis and interpretations, to assist doctors and patients on data results.

- **Green and Renewable Energy**
  o **Building Analyst (Target Industry: Energy Efficiency Assessment)**—Weatherization investments are creating demand for Building Analysts.
  o **Green and Lean Manufacturing**—Lean Manufacturing with "Green" techniques to cuts costs, increase productivity for competitive markets.
  o **Concentrated Solar Power**—Green energy sources (manufacturing and sustainment) that provide energy sources during low or no sunlight

Some Suggestions on Selection Criteria

A selection panel will be used to select participants for the program. Students will be considered for the program based on the following criteria:

1. A grade point average of 2.0 or above
2. Quality of a 500 word essay based on expressed motivation, commitment, stated career interests and reason for wanting to participate in the program
3. Extra-curricular activities or community service
4. Overall application
5. Parental agreement

Competency Development

Teams should align to implement TIGRE programs. The teams will consist of ongoing and proposed workforce-focused requirements, including recruitment, assessment and training. Project Teams will target specific core competencies, at an earlier stage of professional development that historically implemented. Focusing these critical skills and leadership development at a pre-college level will strengthen the candidate's ability to secure and maintain successful career and employment opportunities.

These ten teams will focus on:

1. Team Building—how to surface, diagnose, and work through the issues that impede effective teamwork
   a. Leadership Skills
   b. Communications
   c. Common Goals
   d. Effective Team Elements
   e. Skilled Facilitation Elements
   f. Public Speaking
   g. Laws of Teamwork
   h. Discipline

2. Financial Acumen
   a. Developing and Sustaining Independence
   b. Income and Expense
   c. Household Budget Element
   d. Taxes and Impacts on Income
   e. Wealth Building Strategies
   f. Investments Market Summary
   g. Household Budgeting

3. Business Plan Development (Personal and Professional)
   a. Business Plan Element
   b. Value Proposition
   c. Finding Investors

    d. Selling Your Idea

    e. Funded, what's next?

4. Academic Excellence—Academic programs designed to meet the identified situational needs of students.

    a. Individualized Assessment

    b. Accelerated Learning Tools

    c. Writing Manuals

    d. Mathematics and Science

    e. Critical Thinking

5. Life skills

    a. Advanced Life Coaching and Career Mentor Matching (ALCCMM) model

    b. Relationships and Families

    c. Resolving Conflicts

    d. Wealth Accumulation

    e. Planning for Retirement

6. Customized training and/or pre-apprenticeship training,

    a. Engineering and Technical—

    b. Aerospace (and related) Engineering fields

    c. Traffic Engineering—

    d. Aerospace and Manufacturing

    e. Health Sciences

    f. Green and Renewable Energy

7. Occupation-specific Professionalism

    a. Individual Contributor

    b. Management and Leadership Thinking

    c. Advance Team Building for Leaders

    d. Habits of the Highly Effective

    e. Efficient Record Keeping

8. Career and job placement, retention, state assisted case management and retention support.
   a. Job Hunting
   b. Networking
   c. Resume Building
   d. Scholarship Researching

9. TIGRE Research Project and Proposal (Thesis)
   a. Project and Team Participations
   b. Partnerships
   c. Business Solutions
   d. Inventions (Development and Promotions)

Measurements—Cleary define (and update as appropriate) the barriers to college entry, with a targeted 10% (or similar) improvement in the rate of students attending college after high school, and complete the 4-year degree.

Priority Populations

The Partnership will target at risk and urban youth needing additional skills to qualify for emerging green industry jobs, advancement, and/or high paying jobs. These youth candidates will be screened by the following assessment factors

a. High potential, motivated youths desiring to further skills and knowledge that have limited accesses to existing program
b. Limited of exposure to college, junior college, training and professional programs
c. Likely college-capable students with limited financial resources to support 4-year college program, and
d. Trade and skill capable that have some potential to work with attending school as a method of offsetting tuition costs. Skills they receive will equip applicants with lean and green manufacturing knowledge, as well as hands-on assistance in implementing techniques learned.

In short, there are opportunities for preparing the next generation to have Good Success. This is one. You may have others thoughts that have not been brought to light. Regardless, if we are going to grow as a nation and world community our focus will have to shift from reacting to global economic shortages to new innovations and technology that improve the life and fabric of its people. We must continue to evaluate how we educate and prepare our youth for tomorrow challenges. Population growth, food/housing shortages, transportation, health care, and defense will be at the forefront of tomorrow's jobs.

CHAPTER 5

"Good Success"

CHAPTER 5

"Good Success"

- Dreams into Reality
- Adversities
- Trials and Tribulations

[17] "I know how great this makes you feel, even though you have to put up with every kind of aggravation in the meantime. Pure gold put in the fire comes out of it proved pure; genuine faith put through this suffering comes out proved genuine. When Jesus wraps this all up, it's your faith, not your gold that God will have on display as evidence of his victory."

Glory Just Around the Corner

[18] Friends, when life gets really difficult, don't jump to the conclusion that God isn't on the job. Instead, be glad that you are in the very thick of what Christ experienced. This is a spiritual refining process, with glory just around the corner.

"Good Success" is on the inside of you. God expects us to fulfill our God-given assignment, what you were born to do.

[19] That's why I don't think there's any comparison between the present hard times and the coming good times. The created world itself can hardly wait for what's coming next. Everything in creation is being more or less held back. God reins it in until both creation and all the creatures are ready and can be

released at the same moment into the glorious times ahead. Meanwhile, the joyful anticipation deepens.

[20] *"The God who made the world and everything in it, this Master of sky and land,* well if we are the God created, we should allow God to direct our path *doesn't live in custom-made shrines or need the human race to run errands for him, as if he couldn't take care of himself. He makes the creatures; the creatures don't make him. Starting from scratch, he made the entire human race and made the earth hospitable, with plenty of time and space for living so we could seek after God, and not just grope around in the dark but actually find him. He doesn't play hide-and-seek with us. He's not remote; he's near. We live and move in him, can't get away from him! One of your poets said it well: 'We're the God-created.' Well, if we are the God-created, it doesn't make a lot of sense to think we could hire a sculptor to chisel a god out of stone for us, does it?"*

A S A CITIZEN of the global marketplace, you are tasked with filling a need. Always remember to ask the question: "What was I born to do? What void am I supposed to fill" If you don't know, you need to seek sound counsel, a good relationship with God, regardless of who you are. God wants you to have "Good Success". To be completely honest, the question is worth asking over and over again throughout your life and at every crossroad that you face. It should be a road sign that drives every decision that you are faced with. It should be at the center of gravity that keeps you balanced. It should be the carrot that is held out in front of you which causes you to chase your destiny. This is the garden that He has placed us in.

It is not sitting around waiting for a revelation to fall out of the sky. You must work the work. You need the action in your life. This is why I have noticed that it takes a special personality and skills to bring things to pass. You must have faith, boldness and confidence. You must follow up with action. Consider the story of the ruler and the talents. Watch this time, with an eye on action:

As this story continues, watch this time with an eye on in-action:

Some people look at what others have, or are doing and try and measure their success as a pattern for succeeding. Well I am trying to stir the readers of this book to what' ever is given to you in the area of resources or talent don't hide it or do not allow it to grow or have increase. So much has happen within just the last two decades all over the entire world to all types of people. We are sounding an alarm to people who want to bring change for others and understanding that it automatically brings change for yourself. We call this the 360 business plan.

As a message to others as the author I can say that as of for my life the road wasn't easy, but I made a decision and I had the tenacity to move forward even when banks, and doors close from people that had the resources that could have taken my course a different directions and didn't, but as I continued to move forward I met people that I connected with that mentored me in Business, like my Attorney Edward Burt. Who showed me how to develop and set up all type businesses, my mentor Vincent Spino who showed how set up our 501C(3), all because I was helping others in my state. I did not have lots of money, but I had a lot of ideas as a young lady, in my early teens, I wanted to fill a need and do for others what I saw as a need, that was not yet created or thought of, but it would help people become more successful. As I continued to move forward not looking at what I was lacking but because my motives where pure, more professional divine connections of many wonderful people kept coming into my life to help me help people who wanted to be help.

If you decide to follow this plan, you will not have to fuss about what's on the table at mealtimes or whether the clothes in your closet are in fashion. There is far more to your life than the food you put in your stomach, more to your outer appearance than the clothes you hang on your body. You need not be tied down to a job description; you must create the position that fits you. As we see different companies are right-siding their businesses you may find yourself on the wrong side. This is the time where if you have a job you must take it seriously and be the employee that you want to employ in the future.

Remember the 360 business plan is the future. You become the employer instead of the employee. While you sit at your desk think about how you will do things differently and understand that in order to have a successful Business Plan you have to make tuff decisions, and remember what ever you see that is wrong and not right in your perception or what might even be factual, just use it for your goal to do things different when you become the Founder of the new legacy that you are starting.

Remember If you don't do it, you will never find out, that you are walking in a place that has already been prepared for you, but is every man will have to give an account for what you do and don't do, on earth. Everyone that has a purpose to furfull this is your greatest hour!

Lots of wonderful individuals around this World from all walks of life have been created to do something unique and very special, that will bring change to all of humanity. I am taking this special time with the readers of this book all because of some people have gone through a difficult time and some decision that was made on their behalf have caused them to be in a place of change, for what ever reason. We are here to encourage everyone who wants to be encouraged, but most importantly you deserve to have a fresh start. Don't forget when you rethink about what it is your going to do different, remember the 360 plan of effect it becomes full circle. Now we look inside the full scope of bringing women from all over the world together to help build women, and what we see is that anyone united with the mission of helping empower women in the area of Entrepreneurship gets a fresh start, which will cause untapped wealth to bring a 360 around this Global economy a created new. Most of the old life of the way we use to do things is gone; a new life burgeons! Look at it! WWW.WGECTOUR.COM

We also have a social responsibility
Enough! You've corrupted justice long enough,
*   you've let the wicked get away with murder.*

You're here to defend the defenseless,
*   to make sure that underdogs get a fair break;*
Your job is to stand up for the powerless,

Women are strong and smart, but we are the weaker vessesls, but you will see a rise in women across the globe like never before in the years to come. See our attributes from A-Z.

That's why I don't think there's any comparison between the present hard times and the coming good times. The created world itself can hardly wait for what's coming next. Everything in creation is being more or less held back. God reins it in until both creation and all the creatures are ready and can be released at the same moment into the glorious times ahead. Meanwhile, the joyful anticipation deepens. All around us we observe a pregnant creation. The difficult times of pain throughout the world are simply birth pangs. But it's not only around us; it's within us. The Spirit of God is arousing us within. We're also feeling the birth pangs. These sterile and barren bodies of ours are yearning for full deliverance. That is why waiting does not diminish us, any more than waiting diminishes a pregnant mother. We are enlarged in the waiting. We, of course, don't see what is enlarging us. But the longer we wait, the larger we become, and the more joyful our expectancy.

"Let us make human beings in our image, make them
    reflecting our nature
So they can be responsible for the fish in the sea,
    the birds in the air, the cattle,
And, yes, Earth itself,
    and every animal that moves on the face of Earth."
God created human beings;
    he created them godlike,
Reflecting God's nature.
    He created them male and female.
God blessed them:
    "Prosper! Reproduce! Fill Earth! Take charge!
Be responsible for fish in the sea and birds in the air,
    for every living thing that moves on the face of Earth."

"I've given you
    every sort of seed-bearing plant on Earth
And every kind of fruit-bearing tree,
    given them to you for food.
To all animals and all birds,
    everything that moves and breathes,
I give whatever grows out of the ground for food."
    And there it was.

We must begin to see clearly what we must take our position on the task that has been given to us. Some have a small task and some have a larger task to furfill, but it is all important. We must value the time in which we have to do our part in the earth to bring hope and change that will benefit all of humanity.

Our ultimate goal is to become the funding source for WGEC to not only train women at our virtual global center but also become the funding source, to fund the global business plans for women in business. Our goal is to become the financial institution that will help women after training in the area of economics. We will always be a center of resource for women, in new technology innovation green renewable energy for a global company.

As we mentioned before, we are starting a revolution for women for Good success. As for myself, the financial institution have never given me anything for my business to start up, but I managed to sacrifice and succeed, to the place where I can make it happen for other women, throughout the world. I must say that I have been the recipient of some of my educational training to be paid by a financial institution Also other financial institutions, banks, have funded a major event in my state to help people for the housing crash in the US, a program to assist people in trouble of loosing their home. So nothing against them, it is just that they are holding on to all of what they have and are not doing anything for the masses, especially small business.

WGEC created our 360 business plan to help keep the world economy flowing that when the dust settles, the legacy that we would have instituted will have long lasting effects. The 360 business plan have everyone in mind. It is for the benefit of all humanity of mankind. Good Success will be the story. It is a new day and women all across the globe will start the Good Success revolution. We will be launching soon, so look out for the

"Good Success" will bring and promote:

- Education reformation
- Social Reconstruction
- Community Development
- Political Enfranchisement
- Economic Empowerment
- Spiritual Renewal
- Day Changed Liberation

It regulates and re-aligns the five pillars of society. It imparts every facet of humanity. God wants us to not only have "Good Success", but liberty, empowerment, and inheritance.

"Good Success Stories"

I would like to dedicate this chapter to all of the women that went through the organization of Miss Black Connecticut Scholarship Pageant every young woman that came into this organization since its inception in 1989. I will call each one of them a gold medalist they came from different walks of life. They each went through a six month boot camp experience. They all came in one way but came out of it a different way. They had training for preparation for community networking people and education public speaking interviewing skills, scholarship research, positive interactions, networking imperative building bridges to relationship with influential people, most of all college preparation and research.

The universities that these women attended and graduated at the top of this class Yale, Duke, Brown, Georgetown, Howard, Spellman, Wilbur forest, Hampton, Fordham, UCONN, Southern CT State, Central all of these prestigious universities in the Western region. These young ladies graduated and are now professionals, entrepreneurs, doctors, lawyers, nurses, teachers, financial etc. they are all operating in Good Success around the country.

The organization impacted the lives of these women at a time in when someone had said to them "you can't do it," or "you are not going to amount to anything". But just because they finished what they started, even though they all had a different course to triumph but finished and became what they deserved and dreamt of being are gold medalist and women of "Good Success".

There are a couple of women that mad a lasting impression on my life and I will never forget their story. Dr. Andrea who has become very successful and now helps the women in her community and touched a lot of babies coming into this world, we have not heard the last of her yet. Tira, who has become the protégé for the head of Miss Black Connecticut Scholarship Pageant organization. Kim who is now an attorney, Yale and Georgetown graduate. This young lady is awesome in her own right we will hear from her again soon she is a World changer. Miss. Weaver who is a business woman who is going to shape the nation for helping women. Lakeisha started the women of power network. Déya is a radio personality. Bethany is now a social worker. Kori is in the entertainment industry, Dr. Jarita,

Dr. Alexis, Laquita in Economics, Miss Donietta who is now an RN, she located my sisters and sent a message to me to say that "I made it, because I kept hearing your voice over everyone saying that I could not make it and would not amount to anything, but I heard you say get up you can do it, and I did it tell her Thank you!" Melba, Cookie, Tiffany, Ada, Nicole, Karen, Desiree, Taranesha, Jamila, Chari, Kemmarie, Toye, Alicia, Sharmee, Alicia, Michelle, Tamaria, Kimberely, Nicole, Randi, Gracy, Angie, Shariha, Denice, Tewana, Michelle, Felicia, Darshan, Suzette, Erica, Aisha, Anastasia, Pamela, Sharina, Radiah, Sala, Jeannate, TaTaneisha, Tasha, Michaelle, Kialeena, Marlena, Patrice, Khandice, Katara, Simone, Nekita, Patrice, Andrea, Terraine, Joanne, Shante, Alicia, Janice, Marisa, Pearlene, Tashia, Shariba, and Tamari but many more women who also came through the program.

WGECTOUR has the foundation of helping women from Miss Black Connecticut Scholarship pageant on he to change the world, you, community, and family while benefiting all of humanity, leaving legacies that last. We will tour 50 cities, USA 100 countries helping drive the economic engine while empowering women to be economics sustainable at the same time; helping their regions.

WGECTOUR is an engine of a global virtual center to train, teach, mentor, promote, and empowering this area of entrepreneurs, also find funding and networking mentors, to bridge the gap and benefit and humanity in TIGRE

For more information www.wgectour.com

Women's Global Entrepreneur Conference "Good Success" Tour

1. The Good Success Tour will target each of global hubs to women friendly or by invitation.
2. Each conference will host an entrepreneur competition.
3. Competition winners from each tour will advance to a global stage.
4. The judges will be searching for ideas that will benefit all of humanity, causing an economic revolution.
5. Global competition winners will receive scholarships, funding and resources to help fund their business ideas, along with introductions to investors. All registrant will receive further training, mentoring and coaching in our WGEC locations.

For more information on how to compete visit www.wgectour.com

Marketing, promoting and planning (Economics)

We must teach our generations and cultures of what is and will become the playing field. Go you ALL not some into the world, yes regarding the market place, rise up early and strategize.

Let's go through a journey of Good Success habits for those of you who are listening or reading this book. This journey will be divided into two weeks. Take time to focus on each of these steps in succession.

Success Habits Week One

1. **Week one**

   a. Choose to be Rich, Healthy, Live In Peace
   b. The Necessary Ingredient
      i. Persistence, A Necessary Ingredient
      ii. Persistence
      iii. Nothing shall come to Pass—Benefit to All Humanity
      iv. Rockin' Chair Memories—Retirement Transition
      v. Continual Change, Winds of Change are here
      vi. Prophetic Year—2011, prophetic year

   c. Fortifying the Middle Class, Worldwide—The need for jobs to support the Great Commission
   d. Divine Insights
      i. Begin to write—List five ideas
      ii. God will take care of your needs
      iii. Get Help, Coaching, Role Models
      iv. Take Action
      v. Borders removed; utilize social media, internet, LinkedIN, Facebook, Twitter, etc.
      vi. Hear God with intelligence, ear/eye gates

   e. Write the Vision
      i. Forecast plan
      ii. Intellect of God,
      iii. Find out the Needs of God

   f. Supply and Demand
   g. Stir Up the Gift
      i. What do I need to change
      ii. Does God have a plan for me

2. Today Key Messages

    a. Why Does the World Need Your Ideas

        i. "Good Success" habits—Renew Your Mind

       ii. Community Challenges, Local Church Challenges

     iii. World's Political Unrest

           1. Jobs

           2. Food prices

           3. Population Explosion

      iv. The Harvest is Plenty—US 2011 Global Job Shortages—

           1. Harvest is Plentiful, but the laborers are few

           2. 2030 Metrics—Over 20 Million Job Shortage

           3. Require technical jobs (http://video.management-issues.com/2006/8/24/ research/the-labour-shortage-time-bomb.asp).

       v. Generating Ideas

           1. Find a need and fill it

           2. Look for societal problems

      vi. "Good Success" Model

           1. Impregnation

           2. Birth

           3. "Good Success"

3. Conclusion

God's Promise Of Good Success

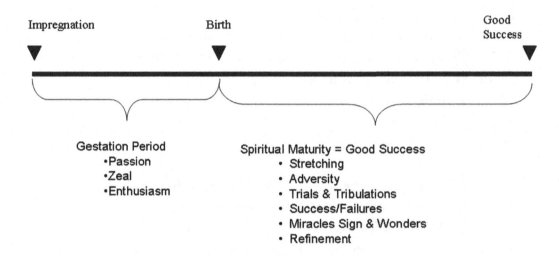

Impregnation   Birth   Good Success

Gestation Period
- Passion
- Zeal
- Enthusiasm

Spiritual Maturity = Good Success
- Stretching
- Adversity
- Trials & Tribulations
- Success/Failures
- Miracles Sign & Wonders
- Refinement

"If God gives such attention to the appearance of wildflowers—most of which are never even seen—don't you think he'll attend to you, take pride in you, do his best for you? What I'm trying to do here is to get you to relax, to not be so preoccupied with getting, so you can respond to God's giving. People who don't know God and the way he works fuss over these things, but you know both God and how he works. Steep your life in God-reality, God-initiative, and God-provisions. Don't worry about missing out. You'll find all your everyday human concerns will be met.

It's comes back to the 360 business plan. You need not worry about finances and having enough. If your work meets the needs of the people you will have more than enough to supply all your needs. It should not be lonely at the top. The true measure of Good Success is if you have done all you can, you have not compromised your morals, and you have helped others along the way. The responsibility of family and leaving a lasting legacy is that the wealth of knowledge does not die with you. When you do the blueprint of your business plan at the end of the day to you have a tangible product and does it meet a need. Some services only last until a better a service comes along. You must stay competitive and make calculated forecasts when you have a product. Lasting services provide solutions and outcomes i.e. doctors, lawyers, and dentists.

Top 20 Wealthiest People 2012

Rank	Name	Net Worth	Industry	Country of Origin
1	Carlos Slim Helu & family	$69 B	telecom	Mexico
2	Bill Gates	$61 B	Microsoft	United States
3	Warren Buffett	$44 B	Berkshire Hathaway	United States
4	Bernard Arnault	$41 B	LVMH	France
5	Amancio Ortega	$37.5 B	Zara	Spain
6	Larry Ellison	$36 B	Oracle	United States
7	Eike Batista	$30 B	mining, oil	Brazil
8	Stefan Persson	$26 B	H&M	Sweden
9	Li Ka-shing	$25.5 B	diversified	Hong Kong
10	Karl Albrecht	$25.4 B	Aldi	Germany
11	Christy Walton & Family	$25.3B	Wal-Mart	United States
12	David Koch	$25B	Diversified	United States
13	Sheldon Adelson	$24.9B	Casinos	United States
14	Liliane Bettencourt	$24 B	L'Oreal	France
15	Jim Walton	$23.7	Wal-Mart	United States
16	Alice Walton	23.3 B	Wal-Mart	United States
17	S. Robinson	$23.1B	Wal-Mart	United States
18	Mukesh Ambani	$22.3	Petrochemicals	India
19	Micheal Bloomberg	$22 B	Bloomberg LP	United States
20	Lakshmi Mittal	$20.7 B	Steel	India

To see a published list of the Top 100 Richest people see:
www.forbes.com/billionaires/list/

I am sure that there are many more people that are throughout this world that is not included on this Forbes top 100 Billionaires list, by choice. Most folks think they can amass a fortune if they are lucky; a relative dies and leaves a huge estate behind, a good tip on the next stocks to buy or having sound careers. You may be surprised to learn that a majority of self-made millionaires in America are first time entrepreneurs or left from a Legacy. The truth, however, is that wealth accumulation starts in the mind. The way you think about riches will determine how much you amass more than any other factor. Your emotions and motivation affects your attitude towards money. This may sound strange but it is the absolute truth. Everything you see in the physical started in the mind. The computer you are using to read this article was first created in the mind. Before you make any meaningful fortune, you will need to completely change your thinking.

We will soon see a new group of billionaires coming up through the ranks. They will be made up of young people in the areas of TIGRE. They are a wealth of knowledge and will soon surpass their predecessors. This generation will be made up of innovative young people, tech savvy, and entrepreneurial in nature.

If you are serious about getting wealthy, you would want to know how the billionaires behave. What really separates them from the ordinary folks? Success in any endeavor comes through repetition. This leads to habit. Billionaires have habits that make it far much easier for them to be wealthy than ordinary people. It means that if you follow their habits to the letter, you have a good chance of becoming wealthy. Some of these habits include the following:

1) Be highly disciplined—Nothing worthwhile can be achieved without discipline. Billionaires are able to set targets and work tirelessly towards attaining the goals. They work regardless of setbacks, obstacles, or whether they feel like it or not.

2) Proactive—be a go-getter, ready to put in the hours to achieve your goals. Nothing can stop you from acquiring wealth. If knowledge or skills are a barrier, learn a new skill.

3) Do things differently—Succeed by inventing new products or new ways of doing business.

4) Control debt and risk—Successful people know that to invest you must take calculated risk. To fund rapid expansion borrowing may be necessary. Consult far and wide before making decisions.

5) Control expenses—Be proud to be an investor and know that if you are to succeed, you will need to control your expenses. Live within your means.

6) Value small bits of success—Small successes come so be aware. Keep these nuggets, and build on them. For the short term setbacks, learn from them, and don't repeat.

7) Maintain relationships—Don't burn any bridges. Whenever there is a disagreement between you and suppliers, employees or customers, ensure that you part with the door still opened for future transactions. Then, maintain good contacts with bankers, major suppliers, key clients, business associates, key leaders and employees.

Let's take a look at the Chart and examine it and make a check list on everything that is important to you, because it all will be necessary for you to bring it into balance.

The survey sheet below the chart will be necessary for you to rate using the metrics form 1-10, to help you meet the sacrifice of beginning your new life and the legacy you are about to begin. Using the metrics scale 1—lowest and 10—highest.

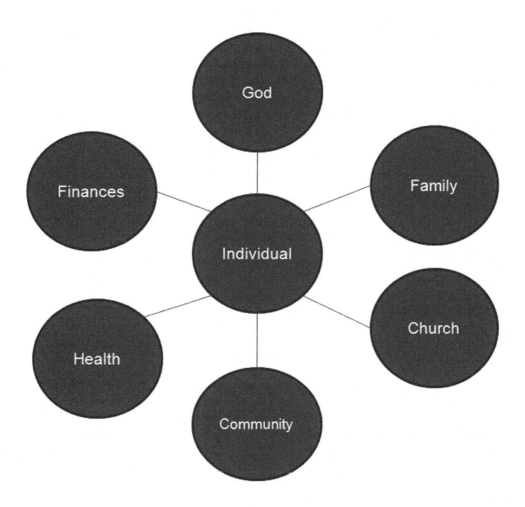

Success Habits	God	Family	Church	Community	Health	Finances
Have passion						
Think big						
Be tenacious						
seek new information and ideas						
Take action						
Learn to negotiate						
Be Competitive						
highly disciplined						
Proactive						
Do things differently						
Control debt and risk						
Control expenses						
Value small bits of success						
Maintain relationships						
Manage Risks						

Let's get started on week II of Success Habits. We have gone through some very important subject matters that some people never consider and often times run into. Some of these could be difficult situations, so as we move forward to the second phase of preparing you for your new endeavor of the beginning stages, we will now take a look into week II of how you start the preparations of developing "Good Success" and positioning yourself to leave Legacy for generations to come.

Success Habits Week II

Success Habits

Part II

Listen to me real good, and read with understanding, as I lay out instructions to help you build a foundation of good success habits. Don't worry about others change your own habits.

1. Part II

    a. Why Does the World Need Your Ideas
       i. **"Good Success" habits—Renew Your Mind**
       ii. **Community Challenges, Local Church Challenges**
       iii. **Key Elements of the World's Political Unrest**
          1. Jobs
          2. Food prices
          3. Population Explosion

       iv. **Prophetic Message; The Harvest is Plenty—US 2030 Global Job** Shortages due to:
          1. Baby Boomers Retiring
          2. Lack of skilled professionals to fill gaps

       v. **Some Wealth Facts**
          1. wealth accumulation starts in the mind
          4. Success in any endeavor comes through repetition
          5. Everything you see in the physical started in the mind

2. Part II

    a. **Prophetic Teachings**
    b. **"Good Success" habits—Renew Your Mind**—what are these habits?
    c. **God and Man Needs your Innovation to fulfill Your**

      i. Purpose for the Earth
     ii. Purpose For Mankind

  d. Break the yoke that holds you—<u>Eliminate Phobias</u>

3. Eliminate Phobia—Set aside all that be

4. Conclusion

  a. Today's Message
  b. Next Week's Message—
  c. Contact Information
      i. Metashar Dillon, CEO WGEC "Good Success Tour"
     ii. Website—www.wgectour.com
    iii. Twitter—WGECGoodSuccessTour
    iv. Email—<u>wgectour@gmail.com</u>
     v. LinkedIn-Metashar Dillon, Women's Global Entrepreneur Conference (group)
    vi. Facebook—WGEC

Now you should be ready to begin your Good Success business plan. Following the steps below you will be prepared to launch.

Cover Page	Should include name, address, and telephone number as well as the names and phone numbers of all the owners or corporate officers.
Executive Summary	The summary of your plan and a statement of your objectives. List your capital needs and how you intend to use the money.
Table of Contents	Is a listing of contents of your plan with the pg. numbers
Organizational Plan	It will conclude a summary a business description, a list of products and services you sell description of your intellectual property, legal structure, management and personnel information, accounting and legal provisions, and insurance considerations and planned security measures.
Marketing Plan	It addresses your marketing analysis, sales, advertising, and public relations campaigns. This plan should include traditional programs and new media (online) ideas. A complete plan should be concluded with customer service, implementation of your strategy and plans for evaluation of marketing effectiveness.
Financials Documents	Projected financial statements, historical statements, and financial statement analysis. Include a cash flow statement, three-year income projection, breakeven analysis, quarterly budget analysis, profit and loss statement, balance sheet and a financial statement analysis ratio summary.
Supporting Documents	This section will include owner/manager resumes, personal financial statements, and articles of incorporation/partnership agreements, legal contracts, lease agreements, copyrights, trademarks and/or patents, letters of reference, demographics, and any other documents important to or in support of your plan.
Application fee	$50.00

If you start thinking to yourselves, "I did all this all by myself. I'm rich. It's all mine!"—well, think again. Remember that the thought was given to you by God, as an inheritance, someone paid an awesome price to successfully lay a foundation for you, so it all came from strength to produce all this wealth so as to understand your legacy or the promise that was made by your ancestors or to begin to understand how to begin a new foundation you must re-think and change to have success habits.

Successful People are

1) Highly disciplined

Nothing worthwhile can be achieved without discipline. Billionaires are able to set targets and work tirelessly towards attaining the goals. They work regardless of setbacks, obstacles, whether they feel like it or not.

It's true that God is all-powerful,
  but he doesn't bully innocent people.
For the wicked, though, it's a different story—
  he doesn't give them the time of day,
  but champions the rights of their victims.
He never takes his eyes off the righteous;
  he honors them lavishly, promotes them endlessly.
When things go badly,
  when affliction and suffering descend,
God tells them where they've gone wrong,
  shows them how their pride has caused their trouble.
He forces them to heed his warning,
  tells them they must repent of their bad life.
If they obey and serve him,
  they'll have a good, long life on easy street.
But if they disobey, they'll be cut down in their prime
  and never know the first thing about life.
Angry people without God pile grievance upon grievance,
  always blaming others for their troubles.
Living it up in sexual excesses,
  virility wasted, they die young.
But those who learn from their suffering,
  God delivers from their suffering.

Successful People are

2) Proactive—Billionaires are confident and go-getters. They are ready to put in a16 hour day to achieve their goals. Nothing can stop them acquiring wealth. If knowledge or skills is putting a barrier they are ready to learn the new craft

> Seize life! Eat bread with gusto,
>> Drink wine with a robust heart.
>> Oh yes—God takes pleasure in your pleasure!
>> Dress festively every morning.
>> Don't skimp on colors and scarves.
>> Relish life with the spouse you love
>> Each and every day of your precarious life.
>> Each day is God's gift. It's all you get in exchange
>> For the hard work of staying alive.
>> Make the most of each one!
>> Whatever turns up, grab it and do it. And heartily!
>> This is your last and only chance at it,
>> For there's neither work to do nor thoughts to think
>> In the company of the dead, where you're most certainly headed

3) Do things differently—Succeed by inventing new products or new ways of doing business.

> the God who builds a road right through the ocean,
>> who carves a path through pounding waves,
> The God who summons horses and chariots and armies—
>> they lie down and then can't get up;
>> they're snuffed out like so many candles:
> "Forget about what's happened;
>> don't keep going over old history.
> Be alert, be present. I'm about to do something brand-new.
>> It's bursting out! Don't you see it?
> There it is! I'm making a road through the desert,
>> rivers in the badlands.

Wild animals will say 'Thank you!'
  —the coyotes and the buzzards—
Because I provided water in the desert,
  rivers through the sun-baked earth,
Drinking water for the people I chose,
    the people I made especially for myself,
    a people custom-made to praise me.

4) Control debt and risk—Successful people know that to invest you must take a calculated risk. To fund rapid expansions borrowing maybe necessary. Consult far and wide before making a decision.

"Suppose one of you wants to build a tower. Won't you first sit down and estimate the cost to see if you have enough money to complete it? For if you lay the foundation and are not able to finish it, everyone who sees it will ridicule you, saying, 'This person began to build and wasn't able to finish.'

"Or suppose a king is about to go to war against another king. Won't he first sit down and consider whether he is able with ten thousand men to oppose the one coming against him with twenty thousand? If he is not able, he will send a delegation while the other is still a long way off and will ask for terms of peace.

5) Control expenses—Be to proud to be an investor, and know that if you are to succeed you need to control expenses. Live within your means.

Buy Without Money
  "Hey there! All who are thirsty,
    come to the water!
Are you penniless?
    Come anyway—buy and eat!
Come, buy your drinks, buy wine and milk.
    Buy without money—everything's free!
Why do you spend your money on junk food,
    your hard-earned cash on cotton candy?
Listen to me, listen well: Eat only the best,

fill yourself with only the finest.
Pay attention, come close now,
   listen carefully to my life-giving, life-nourishing words.
I'm making a lasting covenant commitment with you,
   the same that I made with David: sure, solid, enduring love.
I set him up as a witness to the nations,
   made him a prince and leader of the nations,
And now I'm doing it to you:
   You'll summon nations you've never heard of,
and nations who've never heard of you
   will come running to you

6) Value small bits of success—Small bits of success comes so be aware. Keep these nuggets and build upon them, for the short term setbacks, learn from them and don't repeat them.

   *Ponder and meditate on it day and night, making sure you practice everything written in it. Then you'll get where you're going; then you'll succeed. Haven't I commanded you? Strength! Courage! Don't be timid; don't get discouraged. God, your God, is with you **every step you take**.*"

7) Maintain relationships—Don't burn bridges, When ever there is a disagreement between you and suppliers, employees or customers ensure that you part with the door open for future transactions. Then, maintain good contacts with bankers, major suppliers, key Clients, business associates, and Key Leaders.

Let's Argue This Out
   "Come. Sit down. Let's argue this out."
   This is God's Message:
"If your sins are blood-red,
   they'll be snow-white.
If they're red like crimson,
   they'll be like wool.
If you'll willingly obey,
   you'll feast like kings.

But if you're willful and stubborn,
    you'll die like dogs."
That's right. God says so.

<u>Wealth accumulation starts in the mind</u>

Poverty—Environment

A poverty environment (mind state) is marked with unstable thoughts and interpretations of money. Conditions interpreted as the lack of money create the lack of desire to change and leaves the person vulnerable to poverty conditions. Every day of life is lived within the person's mental environment and it determines the decisions and actions based on what you have or don't have.

A poor mindset will allow a person to view their capacity as limited to what they know to be true, which may (and most times) are not realities. This cycle repeats itself as the person continues decision-making to the point that habits are formed, and are a reality for the person. It allows the person to justify their behavior through continual bad habits and actions.

Wage Slavery

Wage Slavery refers to a situation where a person's livelihood depends on wages rather than investments, gifts or other forms of remuneration, especially when the dependence is total and immediate. The term draws an analogy between slavery and wage labor, and may refer to an "[un]equal bargaining situation between labor and capital", particularly where workers are paid comparatively low wages (e.g. sweatshops), or it may draw similarities between owning and employing a person, which equates the term with a lack of workers' self-management. The latter covers a wider range of employment choices bound by the pressures of a hierarchical social environment e.g. working for a wage not only under threat of starvation or poverty, but also of social stigma or status diminution. (http://en.wikipedia. org/wiki/Wage_slavery)

Personal Shortcoming (Failure)

The most common belief is that a person is poor because of personal traits. These traits cause the person to fail and range from personality characteristics, such as laziness to educational levels.

Success in any endeavor comes through repetition

Social status is the position or rank of a person or group within the society, and can be determined in two ways. One can earn their social status by their own achievements, which is known as achieved status. Alternatively, one can be placed in the stratification system by their inherited position, which is called ascribed status. Ascribed statuses can also be defined as those that are fixed for an individual at birth. Ascribed statuses that exist in all societies include those based upon sex, age, race ethnic group and family background. For example, a person born into a wealthy family characterized by traits such as popularity, talents and high values will have many expectations growing up. Therefore, they are given and taught many social roles as they are socially positioned into a family becoming equipped with all these traits and characteristics. Achieved statuses meaning also what the individual acquires during his or her lifetime as a result of the exercise of knowledge, ability, skill and/ or perseverance. Occupation provides an example of status that may be either ascribed or achieved, it can be achieved by one gaining the right knowledge and skill to become socially positioned into a higher position of that job; building a person's social identity within the occupation. (http://en.wikipedia.org/wiki/Social_status)

Everything you see in the physical started in the mind

A goal or objective is a desired result a person or a system envisions plans and commits to achieve—a personal or organizational desired end-point in some sort of assumed development. Many people endeavor to reach goals within a finite time by setting deadlines.

It is roughly similar to the purpose of aim, the anticipated result which guides reaction, or an end, which is an object, either a physical object or an abstract object, that has intrinsic value.

Goal setting

Goal-setting ideally involves establishing specific, measurable, attainable, realistic and time-targeted objectives. This goal setting can serve as an effective tool for making progress by ensuring that you have a clear awareness of what you must do to achieve or help achieve an objective. On a personal level, the process of setting goals allows people to specify and then work towards their own objectives—most commonly are financial or career-based goals. Goal-setting comprises a major component of personal development. Goals are long or short.

Psychological conditions

In many cases specialists prefer to avoid the suffix—phobia and use more descriptive terms, see, e.g., personality disorders, anxiety disorders, avoidant personality disorder, love-shyness. I would recommend that you go through these phobias and see which, if any, are holding you back from succeeding and getting to the bottom of it. You can be successful and have "Good Success" and remember that your current state does not equal the end state. These are natural, psychological descriptions, which I am not an expert in diagnosing. But they have roots in the spiritual, and I am led by the spirit of God which gives me the discerning ability to see into the bounds that hold you back. With a good relationship with God, these phobias are meaningless. God sent his son so that we may have life and life more abundantly. Nothing will hold us back from that. Set aside some time and spend it praying to the Father. Meditate on his word. Seek his direction for your life and the life of others around you. Categorize these phobias which define the same type of fear. What I do know is that God's perfect love casts out all fear, and sometimes we don't want to come in contact with the unknown which is a part of us all. There is a spark of divinity in every human being and it is a part that some never come in contact with, that part of themselves whether it is because of unbelief or other reasons. The perfect love, of which some don't know, brings you into a relationship with God. This is unknown because of different reasons, but because people from all over the world come from different walks of life. All come in contact with the creator, which breathes the breath of life into our nostrils the same way. So don't let any of these listed phobias creep into your life to stop you from having "Good Success", whoever you are. Check the list and seek professional help if you need it. Check your spiritual connection so that you can prosper.

Eliminate Phobia

To eliminate phobia, set aside all that besets you.

Ablutophobia—fear of bathing, washing, or cleaning.

Acrophobia, Altophobia—fear of heights.

Agoraphobia, Agoraphobia Without History of Panic Disorder—fear of places or events where escape is impossible or when help is unavailable.

Agraphobia—fear of sexual abuse.

Aichmophobia—fear of sharp or pointed objects (such as a needle or knife).

Algophobia—fear of pain.

Agyrophobia—fear of crossing roads.

Androphobia—fear of men.

Anthropophobia—fear of people or being in a company, a form of social phobia.

Anthophobia—fear of flowers.

Aquaphobia—fear of water. Distinct from Hydrophobia, a scientific property that makes chemicals averse to interaction with water, as well as an archaic name for rabies.

Arachnophobia—fear of spiders.

Astraphobia, Astrapophobia, Brontophobia, Keraunophobia—fear of thunder, lightning and storms; especially common in young children.

Atychiphobia—fear of failure

Aviophobia, Aviatophobia—fear of flying.

Bacillophobia, Bacteriophobia, Microbiophobia—fear of microbes and bacteria.

Bathophobia—Fear of depths

Blood-injection-injury type phobia—a DSM-IV subtype of specific phobias

Chorophobia—fear of dancing.

Cibophobia, Sitophobia—aversion to food, synonymous to Anorexia nervosa.

Claustrophobia—fear of having no escape and being closed in.

Coulrophobia—fear of clowns (not restricted to evil clowns).

Decidophobia—fear of making decisions.

Dental phobia, Dentophobia, Odontophobia—fear of dentists and dental procedures

Disposophobia, better known as "compulsive hoarding"—the fear of getting rid of or losing things.

Dysmorphophobia, or body dysmorphic disorder—a phobic obsession with a real or imaginary body defect.

Emetophobia—fear of vomiting.

Ergasiophobia, Ergophobia—fear of work or functioning, or a surgeon's fear of operating.

Ergophobia—fear of work or functioning.

Erotophobia—fear of sexual love or sexual questions.

Erythrophobia—pathological blushing.

Gelotophobia—fear of being laughed at.

Gephyrophobia—fear of bridges.

Genophobia, Coitophobia—fear of sexual intercourse.

Gerascophobia—fear of growing old or aging.

Gerontophobia—fear of growing old, or a hatred or fear of the elderly

Glossophobia—fear of speaking in public or of trying to speak.

Gymnophobia—fear of nudity.

Gynophobia—fear of women.

Halitophobia—fear of bad breath.

Haptephobia—fear of being touched.

Heliophobia—fear of sunlight.

Hemophobia, Haemophobia—fear of blood.

Hexakosioihexekontahexaphobia—fear of the number 666.

Hoplophobia—fear of weapons, specifically firearms (Generally a political term but the clinical phobia is also documented).

Kinemortophobia—fear of the undead specifically zombies.

Koumpounophobia—fear of sewing buttons.

Ligyrophobia—fear of loud noises.

Lipophobia—fear/avoidance of fats in food.

Medication phobia—fear of medications.

Megalophobia—fear of large/oversized objects.

Mysophobia—fear of germs, contamination or dirt.

Necrophobia—fear of death and/or the dead.

Neophobia, Cainophobia, Cainotophobia, Cenophobia, Centophobia, Kainolophobia, Kainophobia—fear of newness, novelty.

Nomophobia—fear of being out of mobile phone contact.

Nosophobia—fear of contracting a disease.

Nosocomephobia—fear of hospitals.

Nyctophobia, Achluophobia, Lygophobia, Scotophobia—fear of darkness.

Oikophobia—fear of home surroundings and household appliances.

Osmophobia, Olfactophobia—fear of smells.

Paraskavedekatriaphobia, Paraskevidekatriaphobia, Friggatriskaidekaphobia—fear of Friday the 13th.

Panphobia—fear of everything or constant fear of an unknown cause.

Phasmophobia—fear of ghosts, spectres or phantasms.

Phagophobia—fear of swallowing.

Pharmacophobia—same as medication phobia.

Phobophobia—fear of having a phobia.

Phonophobia—fear of loud sounds.

Porphyrophobia—fear of the color purple.

Pyrophobia—fear of fire.

Radiophobia—fear of radioactivity or X-rays.

Sociophobia—fear of people or social situations.

Scolionophobia—fear of school.

Scopophobia—fear of being looked at or stared at.

Somniphobia—fear of sleep.

Spectrophobia—fear of mirrors and one's own reflections.

Taphophobia—fear of the grave, or fear of being placed in a grave while still alive.

Technophobia—fear of technology (see also Luddite).

Telephone phobia—fear or reluctance of making or taking phone calls.

Tetraphobia—fear of the number 4.

Thanatophobia—fear of death.

Thermophobia—fear of heat.

Tokophobia—fear of childbirth.

Traumatophobia—a synonym for injury phobia: fear of having an injury.

Triskaidekaphobia, Terdekaphobia—fear of the number 13.

Trypanophobia, Belonephobia, Enetophobia—fear of needles or injections.

Workplace phobia—fear of the workplace.

Xenophobia—fear of strangers, foreigners, or aliens.

CHAPTER 6

The Power of Networking

CHAPTER 6

The Power of Networking

Chapter 6 key Points

- The power of networks and networking
  Putting God First investment club
  Worldwide Networks
- Influence
  You are the light of the world. A city that is set on a hill cannot be hid.
- Leveraging Technology (—Knowledge will increase)

But thou, O Daniel, shut up the words, and seal the book, [even] to the time of the end: many shall run to and fro, and knowledge shall be increased.

This is a confidential report, Daniel, for your eyes and ears only. Keep it secret. Put the book under lock and key until the end. In the interim there is going to be a lot of frantic running around, trying to figure out what's going on.'

DEVELOPMENT—LIFE AND MORE **Abundant Living**—*The thief cometh not, but for to steal, and to kill, and to destroy: I am come that they might have life, and that they might have [it] more abundantly.* It is through this that our influence passes all levels of wealth and status. Why should we live for God? We have a peace of God as children of God that the world doesn't. We have access to benefits from God that is without measure.

These are limitless, as it pertains to benefits from living for God. The world needs these timeless treasures to be unlocked by the word of God and the church.

The church is a community, religious place of worship, where people go to fellowship, fill a need, and for direction. "There came also a multitude [out] of the cities round about unto Jerusalem, bringing sick folks, and them which were vexed with unclean spirits: and they were healed every one." The church is a microcosm, or a small representation, of the Kingdom. It is an organism, a complex system having properties and functions determined not only by the properties and relations of its individual parts, but by the character of the whole that they compose and by the relations of the parts to the whole.

Sustainment—Be A Blessing—A Light on the Hill—We are to be the light of the world. A city that is set on a hill cannot be hid. We are called to be living epistles before men. We are to be set on a hill for all to see. Our lives should be a blessing to others struggling to find their way. We are to leave an impact on humanity that leaves the world better than how it was when we were born into it.

We also know that the church is likened to a legislative body. It impacts and infiltrates territories and implements the foreign policies of its government. Our task is to transfer knowledge to future generations. One of the things we must be trained in, diplomacy, decorum, etiquette and behaviors of an ambassador. We are ambassadors sent into this World. It is our duty as an ambassador the light within the community.

You must have a clear mission. We are called to the nations in this season to seek out those that are lost, and those that are destined to have "Good Success". And lastly, be a blessing for those who can't find their way and have nothing. We are called to be the salt of the Earth, a light on the hill, so that man can see Good Success.

Connecting with the New Generation—In recent years, social media has transformed into a new era of connection. Churches are starting to use sites like Facebook and Twitter in order to stay connected with the body and potential new converts. Facebook is a social networking site that is used to connect family, friends, and business associates; share videos, articles, research, news releases, and to directly connect with members and answer their questions. Use the Facebook site to post questions, opinions, inquire about jobs, and to create a network. Twitter is another social media site. Twitter is great for businesses and keeping in touch with others. LinkedIn is strictly a business professional network. Personally I prefer LinkedIn because you can send personal invitations to business professionals and reach out across the globe connecting with likeminded, goal oriented people.

Reaching the Business World

The earth is the Lord's in the fullest of time securing wealth for your children's children and generations to come. God opens doors no man can shut and closes doors no man can open but this is a divine network that last a lifetime. Reaching the business world is the global marketplace and free enterprise. Politically we would hear people say only do business in America but to have good success you but expand your boundaries and go beyond the borders. We need to teach the next generation how to do business with other countries and cultures. Anyone who speaks against the global marketplace is doing business globally. Money is green all over the world and spends the same way. When one continent is down another is up the economy must continue to balance itself. Money should never be used in a corrupt manner to enslave or devalue anyone, instead it should be used to help empower and benefit all humanity. If you want to stimulate the economy a wealth of knowledge is embodied in the women in your local communities, neighborhoods, and households all over the world. You want an untapped resource that will stimulate the global economy . . . start training women.

Youth

Youth have everything to give and nothing to lose. The revolution is going to begin with them. All they need is guidance, mentoring, leadership, and funding. Your task is to make sure you have a youth component in any business plan you create. If you have inherited a business it is probably already built in. When you leave this earth you must pass the torch and leave a legacy that lasts you can't take it with you. Youth need to be well versed in multiple languages, customs, and cultures. You must expose youth to the business world at an early age so that as they grow up the will be accustomed to the global marketplace interacting with people all over the world from all walks of life. Go to school get an education and be knowledgeable about international business. In this 21st century the youth are going to set the revolution of Entrepreneur Globally in science and technology. See our future of our legacies is going to be the dawn of the new day. We must invest in educating them and mentoring them they are the cutting edge for innovative ideas.

That our sons [may be] as plants grown up in their youth; [that] our daughters [may be] as corner stones, polished [after] the similitude of a palace:

Let no man despise thy youth; but be thou an example of the believers, in word, in conversation, in charity, in spirit, in faith, in purity.

Let no one despise or think less of you because of your youth, but be an example (pattern) for the believers in speech, in conduct, in love, in faith, and in purity.

Teach with Your Life

The Spirit makes it clear that as time goes on, some are going to give up on the faith and chase after demonic illusions put forth by professional liars. These liars have lied so well and for so long that they've lost their capacity for truth.

Stay clear of silly stories that get dressed up as religion. Exercise daily in God—no spiritual flabbiness, please! Workouts in the gymnasium are useful, but a disciplined life in God is far more so, making you fit both today and forever. You can count on this. Take it to heart. This is why we've thrown ourselves into this venture so totally.

Get the word out. Teach all these things. And don't let anyone put you down because you're young. Teach believers with your life: by word, by demeanor, by love, by faith, by integrity. Stay at your post reading Scripture, giving counsel, teaching.

Cultivate these things. Immerse yourself in them. The people will all see you mature right before their eyes! Keep a firm grasp on both your character and your teaching. Don't be diverted.

Mentorship Program

Train up a child in the way he should go: and when he is old, he will not depart from it. Point your kids in the right direction when they're old they won't be lost.

CHAPTER 7

Legacies That Last

CHAPTER 7

Legacies That Last

Chapter 7 Key Points

Avenues for you to walk in "Good Success"

YOU HEAR PEOPLE everywhere talking about "Good Success", but ask yourself how do you measure or define success. Then ask yourself "are you satisfied with what you have done on the earth? Have I left an impact for generations to come? "By leaving legacies to future generations, how wide is your scope? What foundation did you rely upon? Who is your audience? Beyond your family and did it impact others also? Did your family really care about it and call it "Good Success"? Is it me? Money? Things? People that have passed? Can I do my part upon earth to benefit all of humanity? As an individual, what do I have in my hands to bring change? Have I just laid up my wealth, money, knowledge, or Goods? Did I just build structures with my name on it to impact me or other people? Am I selfish? Am I having the right thoughts about why I was born?

Wherever you are, and whomever you're serving to be your God, is the plan you have for "Good Success" and not evil, but to benefit all mankind? Ask yourself who am I? What was I sent on earth to do? In what capacity should I function? How wide is my scope to the whole world? What am I to leave on earth? What are the visions and legacies that will last? How do I measure "Good Success"? Is it just money, wealth, things accomplishments? What is in your mind? Just living from day to day, getting up and going to work?

Making sense of having a job, benefits, and first taking care of my heirs and no more, or is your road narrow or wide and straight? How do you see yourself being a world changer, right where you are? What makes you successful? Do you have the capacity to think outside of the box, like the men Steve Jobs, Bill Gates, Warren Buffet. Do you use Social Media creation sensations like Facebook, Twitter, and Linked in? We always make reference to the wealthy powerful men in the world, but what about the women?

Why were you born? What is your fear of opening up your mind to where you have never gone, before? If this book, "Good Success, and Vision of Legacies That Last", reposition you, then even if you physically can't do it, your mind is still working and it is not too late to bring change that will impact others across the globe. You can raise the floor to the ceiling, the ceiling to the sky, and the sky to the heaven all the way to the end of the earth for someone else and be a world changer. So when your time is up, you are still being because, you have done what you were born to do; "Good Success" is small visions and legacies that last.

We have people that are on the ball about what, why and how people are walking in greatness like, Bill and Melinda Gates, Foundation Day, Band Fen, Warren Buffet, etc. If we can remember what Warren Buffet said:

- Reinvest your profits
- Be willing to be difficult
- Never suck your thumb
- Spell out the deal before you start
- Watch small expenses
- Limit what you borrow
- Be persistent
- Know when to quit
- Assess the risk
- Know what success really means
- It only takes two

Again I say unto you, that if two of you shall agree on earth as touching anything that they shall ask, it shall be done for them of my Father which is in heaven.

"Take this most seriously: A yes on earth is yes in heaven; a no on earth is no in heaven. What you say to one another is eternal. I mean this. When two of you get together on anything at all on earth and make a prayer of it, my Father in heaven goes into action. And when two or three of you are together because of me, you can be sure that I'll be there."

I have experienced and come into contact with so many people who tell me of their individual struggles in making the strides in life on their own. Some of these people seem to not realize the power of networking. God has created us to work together. Realize that the next big breakthrough, no matter how small or large, will have something to do with another person. We are often fearful of beginning new relationships because of past failed ones. We feel that everyone out there is looking out only for themselves.

And five of you shall chase an hundred, and a hundred of you shall put ten thousand to flight: and your enemies shall fall before you by the sword.

"I'll make the country a place of peace—you'll be able to go to sleep at night without fear; I'll get rid of the wild beasts; I'll eliminate war. You'll chase out your enemies and defeat them: Five of you will chase a hundred, and a hundred of you will chase ten thousand and do away with them. I'll give you my full attention: I'll make sure you prosper, make sure you grow in numbers, and keep my covenant with you in good working order. You'll still be eating from last year's harvest when you have to clean out the barns to make room for the new crops.

- Story of the Talents
- Improvements on results—Operating in God's Desired State
- The "Bigger than You" (We need your innovations)

But thou shalt remember the LORD thy God: for [it is] he that giveth thee power to get wealth, which he may establish his covenant which he swear unto thy fathers, as [it is] this day.

If you start thinking to yourselves, "I did all this. And all by myself. I'm rich. It's all mine!"—well, think again. Remember that God, your God, gave you the strength to produce all this wealth so as to confirm the covenant that he promised to your ancestors—as it is today.

Women's Global Entrepreneur Conference
"Good Success" Tour

Vision: Put the mechanisms in place needed for socio-economic change and bring hope to benefit all of humanity.

Mission: To educate women, make available tools and knowledge for self-empowerment, and foster international collaboration between Eastern and Western communities.

Tours: Major US cities and Global Economic Hubs recruiting women across 100 countries.

Scholarships: Receive scholarships, funding and resources to help fund their business ideas, along with introductions to investors. All registrant will receive further training, mentoring and coaching in our WGEC locations.

Areas of Focus:

TIGRE
- Technology
- Innovation
- Green-renewable energy

Education Reformation
- Leaving a legacy that will last
- A plan for the future, as cost goes up for college
- Importance of being educated
- What happens if you are not educated
- Education and women

Social Reconstruction
- Each individual need to take responsibility at home first, to self, spouse, family and then extended family to community, leaving positive legacy that lasts
- Identify your sphere and what you are capable of doing, to help benefit all of humanity
- Redefine your purpose of why you were ever born, and assess yourself.
- Social reconstruction and Women

Community Development
- Take note that if you are already a leader, with resources, then rise up and take a snapshot of your surroundings. You must find a need and fill it, by making a decision to bring change to develop your community.

- Community development and Women
- Leaders that are being developed, you must position yourself, by getting ready to take over, not repeating the things that were not right in your community, but get things in place legally to become a force and a mouthpiece, for all people change lives and issues that does not benefit all of humanity, leaving legacies
- Develop your community

Political Enfranchisement
- Understanding truth when it comes down to parties, up you as an individual, group and nations
- Understanding of political party
- Understanding each parties mission statement, when it comes down to the business community
- Political parties bring term goals concerning economics
- Politics and women leaders

Economic Empowerment
- Economics in its real context
- Economics and women business
- Economics and the Global view

Spiritual Renewal
- What does spiritual renewal mean
- What will it do to help me as an individual, community, and world
- Why do more women search for spiritual renewal
- How can it help you
- What do I do to begin the process

Day Change Liberation
- What is day change liberation
- How can I make a difference
- What can I do to help my family, community or country in a positive way, so we can experience progress?

The Attributes of Good Successful Women
21st Century Leaders

alive
amazing
ambitious
anchors
angles
anointed
attractive
aunts
awesome
beautiful
believer
blessed
brilliant
builders
business owners
capable
caring
champions
Chosen one
classy coacher
cleaners
cleaver
comforters
conquers
considerate
consoler
counselor
courageous
creator
cultivator
cute

dancer
definer
delicate
desirable
developer
diamond
diplomatic
discoverable
dreamer
eagles
encourager
entertainer
entrepreneurs
exceptional
extraordinary
exuberant
fabulous
favored
forgiving
friends
fulfilling
funny laughable
generous
genius
gentle
genuine
gifted
giver
glamorous
global
glorious

go getter
goal setter
gold
gold medalist
Good Successful
graceful
grateful
greatness
hand holders
hard worker
healers
help mates
honesty
honor
hopeful
hospitality
humble
independent
influential
innovator
integral
integrity
intellectual
intelligence
intuitiveness
inventors
jewel
joyous
judge
kind courteous
lady

lady like
legacy holders
life giver
light
lovable
lovers
loving
loyal
magical
majestic
majesty
mentoring pariahs
mentors
merciful
minister
missionary
modest
mother in law
mothers
motivators
movers
mysterious
negotiators
nice
nurturer
nurtures
organizer
overcomes
partners
passionate
peace makers
peculiar
perfectionist
personable
philanthropist

poets
poets
positive
powerful
praise
pray
precious
pretty
princess
problem solvers
professional
prosperous
provider
purpose
queen
quiet
reassuring
receiver
regal
respectful
romantic
royalty
sacrificial
seers
sensitive
serious
servers
service
shakers
short
sincere
singer
sister
smart
soft

sophisticated
spectacular
spiritual
stern
strengthens
strong
successful
survivor
tall
teachers
tenacious
tenacity
tender
thinker
tradeswoman
trailblazers
traveler
trend setters
triumphant
truth seeker
truthful
understanding
unique
universal
valuable
versatile
vibrant
victorious
virtuous
visionary
wisdom
wise
woman
world leader
worthy

writer
zeal
zealous
Zion
zircon

1. Pg. ix   "The Richest Man in Babylon"
2. Pg. xiii   "Tangible ideas into tangible ideas" *Power of Vision,* Metashar Dillon
3. Pg. xiii   A good man leaves an inheritance, Message Bible
4. Pg. 1   So my very dear friends Message Bible
5. Pg. 1   "Don't give up" Message Bible
6. Pg. 2   Magic of the Remote control CNN Josh Levs
7. Pg. 2   "Whoever sows reaps rewards", Message Bible
8. Pg. 5   "It happens so regularly that is't predictable Message Bible
9. Pg. 9   Because of the extravagance of these revelations Message Bible
10. Pg. 9   Once I heard that Message Bible
11. Pg. 11-12   Court trial transcript Savannah, GA
12. Pg. 15   "Focus on yourself and don't worry about what everyone else is doing" Etta Brown Bromell
13. Pg. 17   Harvey Mackay
14. Pg. 17   "There is opportune time to do things" Message Bible
15. Pg. 43   "I know how great this makes you feel" Message Bible
16. Pg. 43   "Friends when life gets really difficult" Message Bible
17. Pg. 43   "That's why I don't think there is any comparison between the present hard times and the coming good times the created world itself can hardly wait for what is coming next" Message Bible
18. Pg. 44   "The God who made the world" Message Bible
19. Pg. 54   "Gods Promise of Good Success Chart Message Power of Vision, Metashar Dillon
20. Pg. 54   "if God gives such attention to the appearance of wildflowers-most of which you have never seen don't you think he'll attend to you" Message Bible
21. Pg. xiii   "A good life gets passed on to grandchildren" Message Bible
22. Pg. 63   "This is what God says the God who builds a road right through the ocean Message Bible
23. Pg. 64   "Suppose one of you want to build a tower won't you first sit down and estimate the cost to see of you have enough money to complete it" Message Bible
24. Pg. 64   "buy without money" Message Bible
25. Pg. 65   "Ponder and meditate on it day and night making sure you practice everything written in it." Message Bible
26. Pg. 65   "let's argue this out" Message Bible

27.   Pg. 66   Definition of Wage Slavery, Wikipedia

28.   Pg. 66-67   Definition of Social Status, Wikipedia

29.   Pg. 68-71   Definition of Phobias, Miriam Webster's Dictionary

30.   Pg. 75   "Ye are the light of the world" Message Bible

31.   Pg. 75   "This is a confidential report" Message Bible

32.   Pg. 75   A city that is set on a hill cannot be hid Message Bible

33.   Pg. 76   We are ambassadors set into this world Message Bible

34.   Pg. 77   That our sons maybe as plants grown up in their youth. Message Bible

35.   Pg. 78   Let no man despise thy youth. Message Bible

36.   Pg. 78   Teach with your life. Message Bible

37.   Pg. 78   Train up a child in the way they should go.

38.   Pg. 82   Reinvest your profits, etc . . . Warren Buffett

39.   Pg. 82   Take this most seriously Message Bible

40.   Pg. 83   I'll make the country a place of piece. Message Bible.

41.   Pg. 83   God giveth the power to get wealth Message Bible

REFERENCES

1) *After the Recovery: Help Needed, The Coming Labor Shortage and How People In Encore Careers Can Help Solve It,* by Barry Bluestone. 2010. *http://www. northeastern.edu/dukakiscenter/documents/EncoreCareersFullReport.pdf*

2) *Employment Trends in the 21st Century, http://www.icpd.org/employment/ Empltrends21century.htm,*

3) *Retiring Baby-Boomers = A Labor Shortage? http://aging.senate.gov/crs/pension36.pdf*

4) *"Labor market Imbalances: Shortages, Surpluses, or What?", Richard B. Freeman, http://www.bos.frb.org/economic/conf/conf51/conf51d.pdf*

5) *Newest Professions, Growing Salaries, by Larry Buhl, http://career-advice.monster. com/job-search/company-industry-research/newest-professions-growing-salaries- hot-jobs/article.aspx*

6) *Obama to business: Bring jobs home, http://money.cnn.com/2012/01/11/news/ economy/obama_jobs_insourcing/*

7) America 2050 (http://www.america2050.org/2011/12/house-high-speed-rail- hearing-missed-the-point.html).

8) *U.S. Loses High-Tech Jobs As R&D Shifts Toward Asia,* http://www.wall streetjournal.de/article/SB10001424052970204468004577167003809336394. html#ixzz1jq6B94y5

9) *CLRsearch.com,* http://www.clrsearch.com/New_Britain_Demographics/CT/ Population-by-Age

10) *Plenty of jobs, if you've got the right skills,* by Anthony Mason, http://www. cbsnews.com/stories/2011/06/14/eveningnews/main20071167.shtml